T0277194

1967

1967

How I Got There and Why I Never Left

ROBYN HITCHCOCK

BROOKLYN, NEW YORK

All rights reserved. No part of this book may be reproduced, stored in a retrieval system, or transmitted in any form, by any means, including mechanical, electronic, photocopying, recording, or otherwise, without the prior written consent of the publisher.

Published by Akashic Books
©2024 Robyn Hitchcock

ISBN: 978-1-63614-206-7
Library of Congress Control Number: 2024935953
Third printing

First published in the United Kingdom by Constable, an imprint of Little, Brown Book Group.

Akashic Books
Instagram, X, Facebook: AkashicBooks
info@akashicbooks.com
www.akashicbooks.com

This book is dedicated to the memory of my parents Joyce and Raymond, who paid for the life I describe in it.

And to the memory of my daughter Maisie, who would have been appalled by almost everything I describe in it: "Dad—that's gross! It wasn't really like that, was it?"

Contents

(Prelude)

So Long, Dalek Sponge

———

I was a different creature then. If I go back far enough it seems as though my life happened to somebody else. I recognize the names I'm writing down, the times and the places I lived in, but I don't recognize the person who actually did the living. He is called what I am still called; we share the same eyes and birth certificate, but I'm not him anymore. Maybe our names should be renewable every ten years, like passports.

Yes, old chap: your memories belong to someone else. They are borrowed from a character in a previous tale who has now vanished. So perhaps you should pass some of his memories on before you vanish too?

Very well, let's try it: who was I? Or, currently: Writing Guy, who are you? That's easy: I am the voice in the head of the person who is writing this. Hmm. Things are getting complicated—let's try another approach: who were you back then?

Okay, Take 2: I was—I am—a twelve-year-old English male who materializes inside a redbrick Victorian fortress one gray dusk in January 1966. There's snow in the air and snow on the ground. It tightens my stomach, remembering this. Look! I am standing in a low-ceilinged room with some other people. A coal fire burns in a tidy fireplace. The scene is cozy. We're ingesting tea and cake through the portals known as our mouths. Most of the other occupants of the room are parents.

Two of these parents are mine: my father, who wears spectacles across his smooth, broad face, and my mother, who doesn't. He has a dark floppy fringe above his brow, she wears her hair in a stylish auburn perm. They are both here nervously surrendering me to the charge of another adult, a teacher named Blotto, who is standing with his Finnish wife. Blotto is in command of this red-brick house. He's bald and genial, with sawn-off front teeth. Between those teeth he clenches a pipe, like a leprechaun might. He has acute brown eyes and a concave nose, like Bob Hope's.

In this cozy room stand two other boys, both age thirteen. The taller is called Horse, the less tall one is called Martz.

Here in the future, the distant future, as I write, Martz's mother is just about to turn ninety-nine. I could contact him right now on this very device—shall I do that? No, better not: that might dilute my focus on this narrative. Not that this narrative is going anywhere drastic, only through time, and for just a little while at that.

So back in January 1966, Horse, Martz, and I have absorbed our nutrients. It's time for our parents to climb into the airlock and eject themselves from the Victorian building. My father leans down and shakes my hand, bestowing an ironic twinkle on me from behind his glasses:

"Good luck, Robyn, dear—I'm sure you'll get on jolly well here."

"Bye-bye, Daddy . . ."

My mother embraces me awkwardly, making no eye contact, but I do get to inhale her pervasive perfume for the last time in six weeks. Then she gives me a penetrating stare that leaves me feeling inadequate, as always:

"Goodbye, my darling; be good and kind and true and brave."

". . . and carrots," I add, under my breath: my mother's attempts to boost my moral fiber always remind me of cooked vegetables, which I can't stand either. "Bye-bye, Mummy."

Then they depart, leaving me to my future. Horse and Martz have been through this before, entering their junior boarding schools, but for the first time in my life I am to be separated from my family and left in a house full of other teenage boys. I will have to take off my clothes and bathe naked in front of them. We will be intimate, whatever that means. I've been anxiously awaiting this for months—being marooned alone in an alien world without anybody I know, or any of my totems. Teresa the comforting Norwegian au pair, my model trams and trolleybuses, my bonsaied dinosaurs, even my turquoise Dalek sponge, have all had to stay back home where my family lives, coincidentally in another Victorian redbrick house about forty miles away through the petite home counties landscape. I don't even have any of my plastic guns—we've been cautioned to bring nothing with us from our previous life.

New inmates aren't allowed to see their families again for at least six weeks, to give us time to adjust our inner compasses. Cell phones and email are still another thirty years off—mere science fiction. In 1966, alone is alone.

Horse, Martz, and I are led through a varnished wooden doorway and down one step into our new life. Our feet land on creaking floorboards, just as astronauts' feet will soon be landing on the moon. There are floorboards everywhere, clonking with the tread of leather shoes. We pass through labyrinths and grottoes of dark timber. There are high ceilings with sad overhead lights striving to beam antique electricity down onto the boys below. Boys swarm everywhere; it seems like hundreds of them, in their shoes and trousers and jackets. I close my eyes and breathe the place in through my twelve-year-old nose. Boot polish. Disinfectant. Burned onions! Nothing that I'm in a hurry to smell, but nothing threatening either. I open my eyes again, and follow the others into a hall. I'm high on dread.

The light is brighter there, and I can see that all around this hall (it's called Hall) are wooden cubicles, varnished like everything seems to be in this house. Each cubicle comprises a desk, a seat, and a lamp. But before anyone can explain anything to us novices comes the thrilling crackle of a stylus on vinyl, and the voices of Paul McCartney and John Lennon erupt from a round metal grille in the only unvarnished piece of wood in the place: "Asked a girl what she wanted to be / She said, Baby, can't you see?" The Beatles have penetrated even here, to the House Gramophone.

"Mudfellow! Turn it down!"

"It is down, you oaf!"

"You—you weren't here last term: what are you called?"

"What am I for?" I ask.

"What are you called? What is your name, new man?" shouts Mudfellow.

"My name?" I blush: "Er, let me think . . . um, yes, er . . . Hitchcock, probably."

They laugh, these taller boys. People are less likely to

attack you if you can make them laugh: that's the first thing that boarding school teaches me. I'd made a joke of being too scared to speak.

The Beatles are faded out halfway through "You Won't See Me." Their latest LP *Rubber Soul* is as new to me as everything else here, though it feels less alien. I am about to spend some quality time with *Rubber Soul* and other new records, courtesy of the home-customized record player that lies embedded in the wall by the fireplace. On the mantelpiece above this fireplace lie the cracked remains of several 45 rpm singles—I pick one up. The label reads "Hoots Mon" by Lord Rockingham's XI.

"Namers!" An adult voice booms from a boy of about seventeen, two years or so older than Mudfellow and his companion, Gallows Senior. I am aware that my voice is still high-pitched and girlish, nowhere near breaking. My feet and other parts of my body aren't fully grown yet: looking at the shoes of the older boys, they're like policemen's boots, bulbous and shiny. The voice continues to read a roll call from a clipboard:

"Wantage?"

"Sum!"

"Brake-Derringer?"

"Sum!"

"Sneed?"

"Sum!"

"Hodgkinson?"

"Sum!"

The names fall from his mouth and swim around our ears until each name's owner replies "Sum," the Latin for "I am." Every night here you have to prove your existence. The roll call continues, and as it does the voices replying "Sum!" grow younger and higher.

"Mudfellow?"

"Sum!"

"Scraper?"

"Sum!"

"Hitchcock? Hitchcock??"

"Oh, er . . . here I am."

"'Sum,' you idiot: you say 'sum,'" hisses a voice in my ear. It belongs to Gallows Junior, who has tight red hair and an angry mask of a face.

"Er, sum—sorry."

Another laugh ripples through the room. Other people's errors are comforting if they don't cost you anything personally. I have already learned to survive being embarrassed at the age of seven when I pissed through my shorts onto the floor because the teacher at my preparatory day school wouldn't let me get up from my desk and go to the toilet.

(Prelude)

Flashback

———

Private education. That's what my parents are paying the big bucks for. My mother's father and uncle were ironmonger's children from the Forest of Dean, on the Welsh border, who made a tidy amount of money inventing and marketing pneumatic tires and central heating systems between the world wars; two ways of moving air around that made modern life more comfortable for those who could afford them. Then they started a bus company.

As a result, just before the Second World War my mother was sent to boarding school and after the war went on to read History at Cambridge University, where she eventually became one of the first generation of women to be allowed to graduate with an official degree.

There, in 1946, she met my father, who had been wounded in his right knee in Normandy, a few weeks after the D-Day landings. Consequently, he couldn't bend his right leg. Before the shrapnel hit him in a forest he'd been an ace sprinter. After nine months in hospital in Gateshead, near Newcastle, he was able to stand up, but he never ran again. Still, he can walk, without even a cane. I'm glad he's not an amputee, at least.

My father graduated from Cambridge with an Engineering degree, and is working for Mercury Satellite Communications in London when I first become aware of him in the mid-1950s. We are living in Weybridge, Surrey, in a semidetached white house opposite a cricket green, next door to the newsagent and tobacconist, Mr. Hagley. Every night, my father comes home from work on the train and changes out of his city garb; then he puts on old clothes and paints pictures from his imagination while listening to the BBC Home Service on the wireless. I lie in bed in the room next door; it's reassuring to hear my dad painting nearby. During the 1950s he brings home a good weekly wage; with the addition of my grandfather's legacy my parents are wealthy enough to pursue an artistic lifestyle and I'm part of that artistic lifestyle. They are both keen to see me go to a place of academic excellence.

As I approach thirteen, I've been insulated from the way the majority of British children grow up. My parents own their house; my sister (she's three years younger than I) and I have attended a series of private nursery and preparatory schools. Preparatory for what, exactly? Well, for grander and more expensive grooming as teenagers. With smaller classes and higher-paid teachers, cocooned in an existence that keeps the world as most people know it away, the privately schooled British child is (theoretically) embedded in the upper seams of British society for life.

That's a detached, academic way of putting it, which itself shows how effective my education turned out to be. My reflexes, my neural pathways, the rat-runs of my brain, and—most crucially—my attitude to other people: all of that is forged and tempered by the schools I attend. And, of course, by my parents.

How do I feel about all this, as 1966 engulfs me? I don't know anything different, I'm not curious or empathic enough to wonder how it feels to be part of the world outside.

I am what would in the twenty-first century be called "on the spectrum": it turns out that I have most of the symptoms of Asperger's, at the high-functioning end of autism.

Still, I'm proud to be accepted into Winchester College, because my elders are pleased with me. I'm precocious, performing mental tricks to impress my mother and my teachers. I've learned to talk above my years.

Winchester College requires its own special entrance exam: in addition to Latin, I've had to learn Classical

Greek to take it. (To this day, whenever I hear "The Last Time" by the Rolling Stones I think of learning Greek.) At the day prep school I attended from age six to twelve, the head teacher was named Colonel Bliss. It was he who taught me ancient Greek, in the course of which he would smoke a pack of unfiltered cigarettes in an afternoon. I would watch the silver smoke curl up like a question mark from his fresh-lit Player's Navy Cut. The smell of combusting tobacco was wonderful for the first forty-five seconds or so. Our school was also in Weybridge, Surrey—by coincidence three of the Beatles moved to the wealthy end of it while I was there.

Colonel Bliss was the first person to plant Aldous Huxley's *The Doors of Perception* in my consciousness. The colonel was a man whose mind led him to many places, most of them wholesome. He was tall, dome-headed, and followed by a flotilla of basset hounds. "The Last Time" was a big hit the month my Greek lessons began, though I doubt that Colonel Bliss himself was familiar with it.

My next Greek tutor, the former Reverend Glebe, turned out to be less wholesome. After I had taken the entrance exam (and passed it—yaysville!) I was entrusted to him on Friday afternoons to boost my ancient Greek up to Winchester College standards. By this time, the Rolling Stones had followed up "The Last Time" with "Satisfaction," which was just unstoppable. These records brought guitar riffs into my life, though I didn't know they were called that then.

Theodore "Teddy" Glebe, meanwhile, was an unfrocked vicar with a florid, pyramid face and an amphibian grin. I never knew how I came to be his pupil: it was one of those done deals of childhood. So every Friday that autumn I had to walk up to his dark, cluttered house, which I instinctively didn't want to enter, as it lurked beneath a monkey-puzzle tree. For the lessons, he sat on my left, with a wineglass and some books—books that made me feel like I could smell the words in them, so musty they were. He liked to get as close to me as he could. He drank rather than smoked. I hadn't had much experience with lonely alcoholics then. When I mentioned to my parents that he had offered me "just a little" glass of champagne (or prosecco?) *at three o'clock* one Friday, my lessons ceased. But whenever I hear the Stones's "Satisfaction," the former Reverend Glebe appears in my head, just stage right of Brian Jones, grinning like a frog.

Oh, what can you remember? It bends itself to suit you, as much as it can: the facts are sleeping in the cellar of memory. You can fish them up, dormant mackerel of the soul, to swim once again in the pond of your consciousness; but somebody else is going to recall those mackerel differently from you.

(Prelude)

Day 1, Take 2

_____

The colonel and the ex-reverend belong back in 1965; returning to January 1966, it's time for bed.

"What do you mean 'Fuckarada'? I'm fucking her as hard as I can."

Knowing laughter follows this punch line—not exactly knowing but eager to please, in a way, as if the listeners were frightened of being caught out, of not laughing enough. I've managed to undress without anybody staring at me, I think, and I'm now lying in the dark in my new pajamas, in a bed in the corner of a large dormitory that holds ten other boys. Horse and Martz are in beds aligning with mine. Farther along in the dark lie inmates who have already known each other awhile. Gallows Junior is there, with Scraper, Harpo, and others whose names will eventually slip over the waterfall in my memory. It's Scraper's turn to tell a joke, which ends with:

"I'm fucking this custard!"

This punch line leaves another crater of knowing

laughter. However, we pubescent males on our horizontal perches have barely begun to have sex with ourselves yet, let alone with a female.

I'm fearful that somebody will ask us new arrivals to throw a joke of our own on the pile. Fortunately nobody does: the other kids are probably just glad to have us as an audience. So after a while we, too, offer up some eager laughter. After another while, exhausted by adapting to this cold new world, I fall asleep.

In case you wondered, this dormitory too is varnished: especially the wooden partitions between the creaky hospital beds in which we sons of privilege will slide each night into oblivion. The partitions give us a whisker of privacy, if not a full beard of it. In our cubicle each of us has a small chest of drawers into which our clothes are mysteriously returned clean each night: the school fees don't include laundry classes. Two years hence, in this very room, I will be listening to the Velvet Underground spinning around on a battery-operated record player.

I don't know if you share this feeling, but I've always imagined that I'll exit this life the way I came, reversing my soul down all the paths that led me here. Not that I will necessarily reverse all the way into my mother's skeletal birth canal as her bones get an earth-tan in the Wiltshire hills. Or back into where my father's cock would be in a Dorset churchyard, for that matter. As I write this, a lifetime later, a light-gray cat with folded-down ears is burrowing into my armpit, while his thunder-gray brother guards my feet. Does any moment in life matter more than this one?

And as I do retrace my steps, perhaps these fragments of time in Winchester will become real to me, instead of borrowed memories. Or maybe *I* will become real to me, before I finally disappear. Or is the real me back there and I'm just his shadow, Hitchcock Senior?

(Prelude)

How Does It Feel?

———

So this is what happened to me on the cusp of childhood and adolescence. It left me with a toddler's soul and a middle-aged mind.

The gray snowy January snows on, as *Rubber Soul* spins in the crucible of teenage carpentry that is the House Gramophone. Initiates to the college have to learn a new language, called "Notions." A bicycle becomes a "bogle," your parents are transformed into "pitch-up," ordinary is "tug," being unprepared is "ex trumps," if you're insolent you're being "spree," and so on. A bathtub is a "swill." Winchester College customizes the English language for its own purposes. Some words like "tardy" for late are just archaic English—but overall Notions most resemble the gay/gypsy/Yiddish/underworld hybrid speak of Polari, which Marty Feldman and Barry Took are currently, in 1966, feeding into the world of light entertainment via BBC Radio's *Round the Horne* comedy show. *(Thirty years on I will occasionally see Marty's widow Loretta drinking and smoking her later days away at Café Largo in West Hollywood.)*

Notions are another arcane booby trap at the entrance to the labyrinth that is Winchester College. If you don't master them in your first two weeks you're in trouble, as is your "tee-jay," the boy who's responsible for teaching them to you, and generally helping you adjust to this parallel world. I've been allocated a helpful, upright tee-jay named Gollygosh, who does everything correctly; he loves classical music and never puts a foot wrong. He's a kindly fellow with a straight back and sensible shoes—I'm lucky to have him: I could have been stuck with Scraper or Gallows Junior.

The weirdest thing about these Notions is that, after all the effort you make to learn them, you aren't supposed to use them in your essays or any of your academic work. So what are they really for?

In years to come I will gradually realize that Notions are part of a Masonic-type bonding process that kicks in sometime after the subject has left the matrix of Winchester College. As the former pupil struggles into middle age, the esoteric language of his school days develops a golden patina, and the aging boy can feel a sentimental bonhomie toward anyone else who has learned it. Who but a recovering Wykehamist (as a pupil of Winchester College is known, after the school's fourteenth-century founder William of Wykeham) would quietly call a toilet a "Fo" or know a particular newsagent on a backstreet as "Sunday Grubbers"?

This is all intentional, of course: the college—like the whole British public school system—was devised to keep the people it processes in a niche of their own. Still, you meet some interesting characters on the way . . .

"I say, Gallows, what do you make of those new doors on the outside Fos?"

"I don't miss watching you shit, Scraper."

One of my lucky breaks in life is to arrive at Winchester the term that doors were finally put on the outside lavatories. They're still freezing, but you can at least freeze in private.

Not everyone is happy with this development; some boys whose fathers attended this institution are reporting that their male parents feel they're being ripped off:

"It was perfectly good for us—and it was good enough for the Roman legionnaires: doors are for sissies."

I wonder what their mothers think?

On the whole, I get off lightly: I'm not beaten up, sodomized, or ritually humiliated by the other inmates. Nobody sticks my head down a toilet bowl, nor am I stripped and mocked. Perhaps my parents aren't getting their money's worth.

Every morning but Sunday, letters from the outside

world appear on the gnarled wooden table in the middle of the Hall. Next to them lie copies of the main British daily newspapers. In the morning, between breakfast and chapel (we eat many cornflakes and sing many hymns), we swirl about, hithering and thithering. We have to wear straw hats to chapel, to our lessons, or if we venture into the town, but we don't have to sleep in them.

A few days after I arrive I'm standing by this table, waiting to see if any mail appears in my mother's lop-sided handwriting or my father's much neater script. The House Gramophone is booming away, playing a stack of 45s—here's the Spencer Davis Group's "Keep on Running"; I like that one, it has a fuzz guitar like the one in "Satisfaction" and has a blue label. Of course, it's not the same blue label as the Rolling Stones: they're on Decca Records, while the Spencer Davis Group are on Fontana. I'm learning the things that matter.

Then on comes an orange-labeled record. I've never heard this vocalist before: it's an American voice. What is this? He seems to emphasize every word he sings—and there are many of them. The music is tumbling and jubilant and churns through the room like a river. The words borne on that river tell the story of a fall from grace, but the mood of the song as a whole is exultant—it's exciting—and it must be a hit record or nobody here would have bought it. The chorus just keeps repeating,

"How does it feel? How does it feel, to be on your own? With no direction home—a complete unknown—like a rolling stone."

I see no letter with my name on it. Scraper farts loudly and three other people applaud: he has his fans. I move out of range, with the voice ringing in my ears. Looking at the orange label afterward (it's called CBS), I see that the voice belongs to a pop artist called Bob Dylan. The song seems to be addressing me personally, marooned in this nest of aliens. I miss my family, my world, my old school. At twelve years and ten months I'm already becoming nostalgic. But I can't go back—time is a one-way ticket.

Time rolls on, picking up fresh passengers and dropping them off at haunted stations. I learn to speak Notions, to bathe in a tin tub in an enamel shower room full of naked boys older than me, to pace the stone and flint byways of the venerable college as it lurks in the side streets of a Hampshire town with its long gray cathedral at the center of everything. I learn to polish the shoes of senior boys, to wash out their pots and pans, and to go and buy them Coca-Cola tins from the designated shops we inmates are allowed to enter. I'm young and I adapt. I'm a good student and I know how to amuse other people, mostly. Sometimes I put on a slight stammer, mimicking Ian Carmichael as Bertie Wooster in the recent BBC TV serialization of P.G. Wodehouse stories: "W-w-well, old chap—I'm f-f-frightfully sorry and all that but I d-d-don't have the foggiest idea, actually."

I turn thirteen in early March as the skies lighten and the nighttime begins to retreat. But whenever that orange record comes on the turntable, my ears prick up like a hound dog's:

"How does it feel? Ah, how does it feel? To be on your own . . ."

Like a child abandoned in the forest who thinks the first creature they see is their new parents, so I—in the course of six weeks or so—convert to Bob Dylan. By the time my family is allowed to visit I'm delighted to see them, particularly Teresa the nice Norwegian au pair and my groovy cousin, the Gerundive. However, my molecular structure has begun to change.

How does it feel, really? It feels lonely and exhilarating—there's a momentum to the life that I've been tipped into. Although it's not leading exactly where it was supposed to lead . . .

I'm sweeping the Hall, as the new inmates do. You start at the bottom, performing menial tasks and being at the beck and call of the older boys. Literally: a seventeen-year-old kid with big policeman feet can lean against the fireplace and holler out "Junior!" The last of the yearlings to reach him has to carry out the task that the big guy assigns him—within reason. It's usually a matter of buying him something—he hands you the money, of course, and he might even tip you sixpence, which will supplement the meager rations that we growing youths are fed.

But I digress: I'm sweeping the Hall . . . ah, but I must first tell you of one other peculiar ritual in the place. The youngest inmate has to wake all the other boys in the house, between 7:15 and 7:50 each weekday morning. And who wakes him? A diminutive man in a white naval jacket and hobnail boots called Mr. Trotter. He hasn't been allotted a first name—it could be Pluto or Claude for all we know—but he is definitely *Mr.* Trotter and not just Trotter. He's a wee bald fellow who scuttles in and out of the dormitory at 7:10 each morning to lightly shake the shoulder of the youngest inmate. Then he clatters back downstairs to embed himself in his subterranean chamber where we boys are forbidden to stray. It is believed to be Mr. Trotter, too, who unlocks the grille into the yard that protects us from the world at night, and vice versa.

As the day begins to burn itself into his newly awakened psyche, the youngest inmate has to wake all those who requested a 7:15 call. However, he mustn't say "seven fifteen" or something bad will happen to him. He must say "Phillips"—that's another Notion. There's a reason for this, although nobody alive can remember now what it was. After Phillips come 7:30, 7:45, and 7:50, all good numerical numbers. Being the youngest inmate, I do this for the first term. It mostly goes well, though there is one older boy, the Hon. Thos. Chandelier, who complains that he was late for breakfast because I haven't woken him.

"But Chandelier, your eminence—may your name be praised by cherubim and seraphim alike—your eyes were open."

"I sleep with my eyes open, Hitchcock."

So, to return to the thread here—I'm sweeping the Hall one dusk in mid-March, around 6:45 p.m. The glow of sunset has faded to a chilly blue that I can see through the high barred windows. We are locked in at 7:15 p.m.—after that the only way out is the front door of our redbrick penitentiary, through Blotto's lair.

As I push the broom around the swirl of casual trash on the floorboards, that voice comes on the House Gramophone again; it's the "How does it feel?" man—Bob Dylan. This time it's a different song, one about Queen Jane. I keep sweeping, and he sings about Mack the Finger and Louie the King and the thousand telephones that don't ring and—

"Hitchcock! Careful with that ruddy broom—my feet are still attached to my legs, you know."

"Er, sorry, Gallows—I thought you were a packet of crisps."

"You thought I was WHAT? Don't be spree to me, you're a junior man."

"I, er, yes . . . uh . . . won't do it again, Gallows."

As I detach myself from my sweeping misdemeanor, the music fades away and for a moment there's just the expectant crackle of a needle in a groove. Then a stately guitar cuts through the trivial evening air, decorated by a kind of flamenco instrumental: and now comes the voice again. Solemn and world-weary, it sings the truth as I have never heard it before: "They're selling postcards of the hanging / They're painting the passports brown / The beauty parlor is filled with sailors." I pause in midsweep and stare up into the last blue dregs of twilight. At one point in the song Cinderella, like me, is sweeping up on . . . it sounds like "Destination Roll." What is this place he's singing about? I can't tell whether he likes it or hates it. Is he trapped there or is it where he wants to go, more than anything? As the song unwinds the broom pulls me over floorboards I've already swept. Twice.

"If a job's worth doing, it's worth doing properly, eh, Hitchcock?" says a face that I'm heedless of. I'm led by my ears, and my ears are magnetized by the cast of characters parading before them as the song unspools. Here's Ophelia, and Romeo, and the Phantom of the Opera, and Einstein, and—are there really electric violins? I guess if there are electric guitars, there can be electric violins. Here comes Doctor Filth, and the Heart Attack Machine, and T. S. Eliot—oh, we've just been reading him in English lessons—but who's this Ezra Pound?

By now the music is pounding, though there are still no drums. Then that delicious, scritchy harmonica cleanses the ears for a wordless verse before the last stanza. "All these people that you mention / Yes, I know them, they're quite lame." The voice sounds so sad, yet in a harsh and gleeful way. I'm not consciously aware of it, but it's the blend of contradictory feelings compressed into that vocal tone that makes it so powerful. It sounds like he's writing to himself, and responding back: it also sounds like wherever this place is, it's the *only* place to be. More harmonica, and then—unlike the previous eight songs on the album that fade out—this one actually ends.

I look around: it's dark outside, and boys are beginning to settle into their cubicles for the evening's study. The gramophone is silent. I lean the broom against the fireplace and pick up the sleeve to scan it quickly before its owner can resleeve the long-playing record. It's a whole LP of Bob Dylan—a WHOLE LP of that voice, beaming out hypnosis from the grooves etched into black vinyl. The front cover photograph shows me Dylan for the first time, sitting in a shiny blue shirt looking enigmatically out at life. He looks calmly furious, beneath a lacquer of indifference. But he also looks like he understands that, on some level, everything is a joke. He looks wise. Wise and dangerous.

Unbeknownst to me, I'm now joining the millions of people who project onto Bob Dylan. The record itself is entitled *Highway 61 Revisited* and starts with the song that has become my breakfast-time mantra, "Like a Rolling Stone." It contains eight whole other songs by That Voice—this is the closest I've yet come to the Holy Grail. I study the track listing: there it is, the last and longest song, all eleven minutes and eighteen seconds of it . . .

I have to go to "Desolation Row."

(Prelude)

Flashback 2

———

Looking back, I can see that my parents tried to construct earthly paradises. In the summer of 1967 they will move from one attempted earthly paradise to another.

"Ah, now look at this," my father exclaims, one afternoon in April 1966, while I'm home from my first term away. He's at the dining room table, leafing through the property section of the *Sunday Times*: "My love—this one's a bargain—it's a disused mill that was in the Domesday Book."

"Mmm. Mmm," replies my mother, sitting opposite him, deep in the book review section: "Is it in the phone book, too?"

"Darling, lovey—it's been a ruin since before the phone was invented, so it's a perfect opportunity for renovation . . ."

"Mmm. Mmm." My mother is trying to disappear into the newspaper, but my father persists:

"Just think, sweetheart—we'd be over a stream . . ."

"Yes, but streams are wet, and wet means damp." Mum has finally lowered her paper, taken off her stylish blue winged reading glasses, and is staring directly at Dad like a mad owl: "And you know how long it took us to heat *this* place, darling."

Like many long-term couples, my parents use endearments as weapons. Any sentence beginning or ending with "darling," "lovey," or "sweetheart" is liable to be a rebuke.

"But, my love, use your imagination, for once, if you have one," says my father, bringing out the big guns: "It would only take a year or so, and Brian could probably design it with me."

"Mmm," says Mum, putting her glasses back on and picking up the paper: "Since when were you friends with Brian, lovey? You always said he was a frightful bore."

"Er, hmm, well, you know," says Dad, picking up his part of the paper. "And of course you'd only be three miles away from Robyn when he's back at school . . ."

My mother says nothing for a while, then clears her throat:

"Er, would people like to make a pot of tea, do you think?"

In 1962 my parents left the little white house on the cricket green and moved us into their next paradise, a redbrick mansion on a hill in Surrey, about thirty miles from London. When 1967 dawns, we are still there. It's cold—too spacious to heat. Outside my bedroom window lies a big black square oil tank. Every so often a military-type vehicle comes grinding up the hill and fills the tank with oil. This replenishes the central heating which, when fired up, dissipates through the house and out of the many single-glazed windows.

Only one room in the house is guaranteed to stay warm, and that's the Aga Room, directly below my bedroom. The cream-colored cast-iron Aga cooking range also feeds on oil and radiates heat into this sun-free room with its strip lighting and its shiny-blue linoleum floor. During the winter the whole family huddles in there. I stared long and hard at this blue floor in 1963 when the news of President Kennedy's assassination came through on my father's hefty transistor radio.

"Ooh my," said my grandma. "What did they want to kill him for? He was one of the nice-looking ones." Grandma is my father's widowed mother—she lives alone in the attic.

There's an oblong room tacked on to this Aga Room, called the Parlor: it's the Parlor roof that supports the big black oil tank. In the Parlor lives a black-and-white television. My sister and I were watching a science-fiction puppet show one Sunday afternoon in May 1963 when my father lurched in with his radio.

"Y'all might want to listen to this," he said, "it's the Top Twenty," and he lurched out again, leaving the radio on the windowsill. *(My father didn't use the expression "y'all," but as someone who's been based in Nashville for a while, I know that's what he meant to say.)* For a few confused minutes my sister and I watched the TV and listened to the radio simultaneously. Then on came a haunting song called "Rhythm of the Rain" by the Cascades, so we turned the sound down on the television and listened to the music pouring out of our dad's wireless. *Pick of the Pops* was the only show on BBC Radio that was guaranteed to play hit records. If you weren't in the Top Twenty you weren't a hit. *(None of my records to this day have ever been anywhere near the Top Twenty—indie rock hadn't been invented then.)*

The disc jockey had a UK version of an excited voice: a British accent with an American inflection. "And DOWN two places to number thirteen, it's Buddy Holly." My sister and I had no way of knowing that Buddy Holly had died in a plane crash in 1959—after all, he was still having hits in 1963.

"And, pop-pickers, it's UP FOUR places to number THREE for Jet Harris and Tony Meehan . . ." Hysterical excitement was infusing the DJ's voice. Then from the radio burst forth an exhilarating guitar instrumental that made me think of cowboys on a beach, racing their horses through the surf as it broke on the shore. On the muted TV screen, meanwhile, a couple of puppet astronauts were landing a wobbly rocket in a blast of silent smoke. Outside the window the fresh green leaves of May stretched away to the abandoned pigsties and over to the nearby forest that ran all the way down the hill to a small airstrip that had lain there since the Second World War.

"And HEY, pop-pickers: they're STILL at number one . . ." The DJ was peaking, he'd taken us to the top of the hit parade and here were—the Beatles!

Through the amber of sixty years the Beatles glow ever brighter: they mean as much to me now as a white-haired pensioner as they did to the ten-year-old 70 percent–grown me. To me, and to millions of other people about whom I know nothing except that we'll all be gone soon.

The following Sunday afternoon, my sister and I skipped the TV program and lowered our father's radio into an old pram, which we wheeled around the derelict farmland surrounding our house. Adrenaline buzzed through us as the DJ counted down to number one, which was still—the Beatles!

1967 At Last!

———

Fast forward to January 1967, and I'm 90 percent grown, heading for fourteen years of age, and sitting in the Parlor with my mother's mother, known to us all as Granny. She's a skinny woman with a skull-like face and legs that are permanently bandaged. A benign Egyptian mummy who vibes like a grasshopper.

I like Granny. She has always been simpatico: she loves children, brings us chicken sandwiches in bed, and is a devout churchgoer. She is based out west by the banks of the River Severn where all my mother's family live; right by the Forest of Dean. I'm not aware of this but she has only six months to live. She may be more aware of this than I am. She's sitting back in a maroon armchair listening to a Bob Dylan record that I am playing her. Her eyes are closed and she's tapping one of her bony knees with her thin fingers. "Don't Think Twice, It's All Right" ends and the needle lifts itself off the orange-labeled 45 rpm extended-play record that I've played every day since I received it at Christmas:

"'I gave her my heart but she wanted my soul.' Hmm, that's nice," says Granny, opening her eyes. "Oh yes, jolly good—well done!"

I'm impressed that this eighty-five-year-old English countrywoman can actually sit and listen to Bob Dylan. He's more than either of my more sophisticated parents can take: something about his sound disqualifies most of the older generation from enjoying him. I let Granny escape back to the world of cold mince pies and iced turkey. I slip away up the dingy back stairs to my room, with its black linoleum floor. It's pockmarked where I've focused the sun's rays through a magnifying glass to burn little holes. Outside the window, in the thicket of trees behind the oil tank, I have burned ants and grasshoppers too, alive, also with a magnifying glass, or sometimes just with matches. Storing up bad karma. By January 1967 I've grown out of that kind of violence—now, if it comes, it's directed at myself.

Upstairs in my room I gloat over my things. I finally have my own copy of *Highway 61 Revisited*, a couple of Bob Dylan EPs with shiny color sleeves, and a copy of the first Bert Jansch LP that my mother has thoughtfully procured for me from Dobell's Folk & Blues record shop in London. My mother is very good like that— she's good with gifts. She's not good at making eye contact and she's kind of smothering, though not in a way I could describe. I feel closer to her than to my father but that will change soon. For Christmas she has given him a copy of the first Incredible String Band record, but they have too much of Dylan's attitude for my father to enjoy them.

My father loves traditional folk music. He lay in a hospital bed for nine months up in Gateshead at the end of the Second World War, preparing to enter the world anew as a twenty-three-year-old man with a shattered leg. One of his few joys was hearing the young nurses singing traditional Geordie songs, handed down from their ancestors. His libido must have quivered at the sound of them serenading the ward with tales of the Lambton Worm, Cushy Butterfield, and the Blaydon Races. Years later, as a husband and father (ah, but how he must have wanted our mother, before he and she were wed!), he has collected those songs and many more on a slew of records that are played alongside the Beatles in our chilly hilltop house.

We also have LPs by the Clancy Brothers, a slightly theatrical troupe of Irishmen who sing traditional songs in their knitted white sweaters; they, too, are on the same orange record label as Bob Dylan, CBS. I wonder if CBS is an automatic sign of quality?

Not only am I taller and hairier than I was the previous January, my molecular structure has continued to transform in the year since I first reached Winchester. I'm now fairly happy to go back to the college for the new term: when I get there I'll have enough money to don my straw hat, stride into town, and buy my first copy of *Bringing It All Back Home*, the LP that Bob Dylan released before *Highway 61*. I know these things. They are what matters to me now.

When I stay at Granny's house by the River Severn a week into 1967, I'm starting to write song lyrics: gauche, pseudo-Dylan couplets that fit over the meter of his songs.

"Well I guess, Anne Boleyn, we've reached the end of the line / Maybe we can get together and discuss Nietzsche some other time" is my idea of an extra verse for "Just Like Tom Thumb's Blues." I carry my two LPs around with me everywhere in case I find a gramophone.

My family is no longer my prime source of comfort—although, in truth, I've been relying on a tiny plastic dinosaur and a couple of miniaturized trams as my safety blanket since I was about ten. Until I went away to boarding school I never left home without one, and wouldn't stay overnight in someone else's house unless I had my triceratops in my pocket. Yes indeed.

My heart has become a shrine to the American, Bob Dylan. Being back in the college, slowly creeping up the ladder of seniority starts to feel almost comfortable; there are more kids with records there. If only there was more food to eat.

Like my father, I have always drawn pictures and, being a compulsive child, if ever I drew a man, I drew him with a weapon—usually a gun. I felt that he wouldn't be a real man without one. By January 1967 the gun has metamorphosed into a guitar. And the men in my drawings are beginning to have long, curly hair. They inhabit wastelands conjured from DC Comics and Hieronymus Bosch, my two favorite visual art worlds at the time. But woozy op-art backdrops are also appearing and by the end of the year I will have gone full faux art nouveau.

Sitting in front of a gramophone and drawing pictures is my default setting as I enter my teens. Sports frighten me—those hurtling spheres can hit you in the face. A seven-year-old boy was killed by a flying cricket ball at my first school. I hadn't liked him very much though . . . but then, did he have any reason to like *me*?

So I sit, and draw, and listen.

It's a Guitar, Darling

———

I've been anxious for my voice to drop, to develop significant body hair, and to vacate the squeaky realm of boyhood. Yet the change I crave comes over me so gradually that I hardly notice it.

Martz and Horse and I, along with Scraper, Gallows, Harpo, Mudfellow, and the other inmates of G House, are in just one of eleven hives of teenage boys. Ten of them are giant redbrick buildings rising out of the mossy flint walls that line the Winchester backstreets; the eleventh hive is in a medieval courtyard that was the heart of the original college when it was founded nearly six hundred years ago. This ancient place, perhaps confusingly, is known as "College." Its inmates wear black gowns but no straw hats, and they appear to sleep either on straw pallets or hanging upside down from the wooden rafters. These College Scholars are great minds on legs: they have all passed an exam which, if they score highly enough, gives them—i.e., their parents—their lodging and tuition for free. They enter the school in the high-achieving classes and skip the lower ones. Many of them have mothers and fathers who are academics.

Our classrooms are ranged around a flint courtyard, known as Flint Court. Only the teachers and the boys who have been inmates for more than four years are allowed to set foot on Flint Court itself, so it's often empty. Everyone else must edge along the pavement on the perimeter, as if it were a swimming pool. The teachers also have to wear black gowns to classes, though they don't sleep upside down in them. Those of them who, like Blotto, are wardens of their own houses ("housemasters") have names such as Bloaty, Dopey, Rubber-Lips, the Chimp, and Gazebo. Most of them are married—I lack the empathy to wonder what kind of exotic hell the wives of these teachers feel they have entered. One young teacher, Mr. Felix, has a beautiful wife called Morgana— many of the boys fancy her. To us, almost everyone over thirty is just gray sludge.

Only one housemaster is unmarried. He attended the college himself in the 1940s and returned there to teach in his own version of adulthood. He is called the Shoveler and he's been known to shower naked with the boys in his house after football. I don't know if the boys' parents have to pay extra for this . . . or possibly receive a discount?

The Shoveler is a younger version of several fungal old

men who haunt the streets around the college: they have names like the Bobber, the Dicker, and the Bin. We see them from time to time, tottering out of the school book-shop or hobbling into the teachers' pub, the Wykeham Arms. We see the Dicker's watery blue eyes and slack mouth. They're the senile remains of boys who attended the school in the late nineteenth century and then went back there to teach; eventually they were retired but still they couldn't get away. It's the addictive nature of Win-chester College that causes some fragile souls to never attain escape velocity from it. *(In a way the older me, who will write this story at the other end of my lifetime, is like that: though it's not just the college that will keep me teth-ered to 1967.)*

A year has shown me the two opposing strands in our academy: the meatheads and the groovers. The meat-heads are into sports, alcohol, talking about sex, and the Beach Boys. The groovers favor Beat poetry, jazz, and incense sticks; they're also more likely to enjoy Bob Dylan, and their compass points to hashish. The Beat-les and other hitmakers occupy the middle ground. But during 1966 I have observed a gradual shift: the groovers begin to discard jazz in favor of Dylan, and when "Good Vibrations" by the Beach Boys appears that winter, they actually endorse it.

"But it's the Beach Boys, man," I say to the fully developed seventeen-year-old groover who brings a copy of this single around from Gazebo's house to play to his counterparts here in ours: "The Beach Boys are for all these beerfucker types, you know—the meatheads—aren't they?"

"No, man, you've gotta dig it: the Beach Boys are cool now—this stuff is beautiful, man. It's like jazz with voices, you know?"

Come January and February 1967 the melting process continues—both sides now play Dylan, the Beatles, the Beach Boys (*Pet Sounds* onward), and, of course: whatever somebody manages to play on the House Gramophone, everybody has to listen to it.

"Now who's this American you've got us listening to, Hitchcock?" drawls Mudfellow from his cubicle in the Hall: "Remind me, please, why don't you . . ."

"Er, well . . . it's Bob Dylan, Mudfellow—actually, I've played another of his records today as well."

"You don't say," replies Mudfellow with deep sarcasm, returning his gaze to a fishing magazine, *Trout Quarterly*.

We aren't allowed radios but I've snuck a small transistor into my cupboard and occasionally take it downstairs to the Boot Room where I can listen quietly to the Top Twenty on Sunday afternoons like I began to with my sister when John Kennedy was still alive. It's there, right next door to Mr. Trotter's lair, in a windowless cube lit by a single weak lightbulb, that I first hear "Strawberry Fields Forever." The boots emit a consistent aroma—nothing too rank, but they offer up a musky bouquet that tends to lodge in the back of the nose. The DJ comes on the radio, all the way from the BBC in the Outside World:

"And, pop-pickers, they're STILL at number two." Then John Lennon's voice seeps out of the little circular speaker grille. Already nasal, through my radio at clandestine volume he sounds like an ant, if ants could sing. "Let me take you down, cos I'm going to . . . Strawberry Fields / Nothing is real." The Beatles are developing so fast, and yet, because my friends and I are developing too, this seems only natural.

When this new Beatles single finally reaches the House Gramophone, the groovers endorse it heavily. They lean toward "Strawberry Fields" while the meatheads favor the other A-side, "Penny Lane," but there's not a lot in it: the Beatles are universal. I like "Penny Lane," although it doesn't move me much; maybe it's more about the production than the songs? Not that we're listening in high fidelity, of course.

What's going on elsewhere in the curriculum, you may wonder: are my parents spending all that money on me just to listen to records? The short answer is yes, in my case; but we inmates also study French, English,

German, Latin, Mathematics, Physics, Chemistry, Biology, barbaric sports, masturbation, and under-eating. The other big musical influence on me is the chapel.

Every single morning—and twice on Saturdays—the entire school is mobilized and sent to chapel at 9 a.m. The chapel itself is a fifteenth-century church set on one side of the central court of the old college, where the clever bat-boys hang. The chapel isn't big enough to contain the whole school so the younger inmates are sent into a bijou church in the middle of an old and dusty cloister—it's called Chantry. Memorials carved in neoclassical marble and granite line the cloister walls: memorials to high-achieving old boys who have long been dust themselves.

The bells ring loudly, peal across the flint and brick and stone of imposing English dismalia. We boys drain out of our hives, full of cornflakes and watery scrambled eggs, and file into the chapel as the bells slow down. You must not miss chapel. You must not be late for chapel. Here it comes . . .

My parents aren't people of faith. Their creed is doubt and uncertainty. If you pushed either of them for an answer they would probably both say they weren't sure, that they really didn't know, darling. As sensitive children of the First World War who came of age in the Second World War, this makes sense: after the Blitz, the

Holocaust, the obliteration of Hiroshima and Nagasaki, plus two bloody wars in Western Europe and around the world, what is there to have faith in? My father describes himself as an architectural Christian—he loves old medieval cathedrals, such as the one in Winchester. My mother goes to Quaker meetings in an effort to "try to be a better person, lovey," but she can't muster the certainty of God's love that sustains her own mother: she's read too many books. The only time we as a family go to church is with her parents, up beside the Severn. I personally rejected Christianity at about the age of five because it felt creepy: I felt uncomfortable kneeling and praying to a man in a white robe with a circle over his head. Furthermore, he didn't carry a weapon . . .

Winchester College does not breed faith either; nonetheless, it has a rigid system of worship. All boys (and a fair crop of the teachers) must attend chapel, every day, for reasons that are murky but implacable. I resent the worship, and I don't recite the prayers. But the hymns: what a cornucopia of tunes! Along with contemporary pop hits the college is bringing a lot of old British melodies into my life. Some are twee and some are dreary, but the strong ones will stay with me forever: "Guide Me O Thou Great Redeemer," "Eternal Father, Quick to Save," "Immortal, Invisible, God Only Wise," "The Day Thou Gavest, Lord, Is Ended," and "Jerusalem" are up there with "Desolation Row" and "Strawberry Fields" as fabulous, permanent songs. Fragments of hymns will come to light in my head in the years ahead, like pieces of ancient weaponry surfacing in a plowed field.

Looking down from the future I see the archaeological ruins of 1967. So much of it is lost now; all I can do is uncover a few more of the pieces that are visible so I can assemble some kind of collage. There's very little evidence now of any of this.

It's February and I'm growing still taller; we all are. Some boys crack their voices and shatter into their fully developed frames overnight, it seems. Martz and I slide into puberty, just as years later we will slide into old age. Right before my fourteenth birthday there's a weekend holiday, which means everybody gets to go home for three nights and then the semester resumes. Of course, even without us inmates there to witness them, the staff of the academy continue to live out their lives. But for three mornings Mr. Trotter no longer has to clump upstairs from his den by the Boot Room and wake the youngest boy in the house.

However, perhaps he wakes up automatically and clatters around the deserted building, roaming the empty dormitories as a reflex; or perhaps he goes to stay with his sister, Belle Trotter, who might have lodgings down the road in Southampton. From there, they could take a ferry to the Isle of Wight, possibly accompanied by Belle's friend Alice, where they could spend a couple of grim nights in a bed-and-breakfast. Mr. Trotter himself might enjoy a flutter at the races, or he may prefer to look for fossils on the cliff tops and the beaches of the South Wight, clambering over the rocks in his hobnail boots. The seaside air is bracing in February, and the fossils are plentiful. I picture Alice as taller than the Trotters, perhaps an extrovert who can make the petite siblings laugh and "bring them out of themselves." Possibly, though, after a couple of light ales, Mr. Trotter makes the ladies guffaw with his diabolical imitation of the sleeping boy whom he must wake each day:

"And then, you know, Alice: you know what he has to do, once I've woke him?"

"Naaaaooooow go on, Pluto—what do they do?"

"Oh, this'll kill yer, Alice," hisses Belle as she clutches her friend's elbow. "Go on, Pluto, you tell her what you told me."

"He gets up and walks to the nearest bed next to him and bends down and he shakes this near boy and he whispers . . ."

But here Mr. Trotter is so overcome with silent laughter that he is rocking back and forth in his chair, perhaps in a well-cut if threadbare pin-striped jacket:

"He says . . . he says . . ."

"I thought you said he was whispering?" interjects Alice.

"Phil . . . Phil . . . Phe—huh—huh—huh." Mr. Trotter is weeping with laughter, but finally manages to hawk out the word intact: "Phillips."

He cradles the snuffling dome of his forehead in his hands while Alice shakes her head and gazes out at the lights of Portsmouth across the Solent. Then she turns her head toward the sandwich counter of the little pub they're in:

"I dunno, Pluto—it takes all sorts, doesn't it? Now, who wants cheese and tomato, and who wants ham? There's a pot of mustard I can see up there . . ."

There's no way of knowing if this is happening or not; and from fifty-five years away in the future, there's no way of proving or disproving the existence of any of these people.

So at the very end of February I get home for the weekend, and discover that—could it really be? O stars of joy: a guitar is lying on my bed! My parents have acknowledged the change in me and from somewhere purchased a cheap but functional nylon-stringed guitar. A guitar! My own guitar! I pick it up in my fingers and turn it over. It's a complete guitar. I've never handled one before.

My groovy cousin the Gerundive has one, but I've never been as close as this to it. I have no idea how to get it in tune, but eventually I take it over to the gramophone and begin gently picking away at the strings while my new Bert Jansch LP plays.

My parents, as I've said already, are good with gifts. My mother has been supplying me with colored neckties and natty shirts for a while. It will be six months before I learn to tune the guitar, but it becomes my constant companion while I'm at home.

I take my parents and my education for granted; I am given few responsibilities. I know I will have to do something when I grow up, but there is no indication what, as yet. There is just this guitar, lying on my bed. It doesn't even have a case, and I don't even notice.

Down the linoleum stairs from where I used to burn holes with sunlight through a magnifying glass is a big hall, off which various rooms lead. One is a chilly dining room that looks out over the lawn. In the autumn, giant white puffballs grow on the lawn: breathing fungus, my sister and I call them. This lawn slopes down toward the airfield behind the trees: you can't quite see it but you can hear the small planes taking off and landing.

One January evening I hear one crash in the woods; the noise is over very fast so I don't realize what's happened until the next day.

The room directly across the hall is my father's studio. Sometimes I imagine his skeleton sitting in front of his easel, painting a large canvas with brightly colored patterns. His stiff right leg juts out from the bottom of his smock as he mixes the paints on the palette through which his bony thumb protrudes.

The living version of my father wears a cravat and always feels a bit awkward when I come and speak to him. He's been living mostly off my mother's money for the last few years, though he does attend communication conferences overseas sometimes, apparently. He paints pictures that don't sell, and is drifting across his skill set in search of his most compulsive talent. He trained as a communications engineer (what is a communications engineer?) then started drawing cartoons, many of which were published in magazines. From there he started painting pictures: what might now be called primitive art. Creatures in stony landscapes, basking beneath black suns; women staring out from ruined walls, body parts on beaches; even the commuters that he depicted on a tube train with their pink newspapers, he made them look unearthly. My father painted his nightmares. Post-traumatic stress disorder wasn't recognized yet.

The intensity in these pictures encouraged my mother to suggest that he painted full-time: she had enough money to support them both—why not? Unfortunately, when he went professional, my father began to fall into the thrall of other artists: his paintings began to express Francis Bacon or Jackson Pollock rather than himself.

Sitting in a big room in a cold house on top of a hill three miles from the nearest town, he's beginning to feel emasculated. And my mother's beginning to feel cut off. She likes to see other people and, as my father often points out, he doesn't. He's what would now be called a man-child: wants to be the center of her world, takes all his fears and anxieties to her, and he's jealous of other people's claims on her attention. Including mine.

Sayonara, Pigsties

———

Our hilltop earthly paradise was haunted by God knows what. It had servants' quarters in the attic, accessible by a back door and a discreet staircase. I used to go up there at dusk and sit in an empty room till I wanted to scream; then I would hurtle down the stairs again. Eventually my father's mother—Grandma (the Shuffler, as he sometimes called her)—was installed up there among the ghosts. She was from their generation, after all. But she was, as she often pointed out, rather too old for all those stairs.

"Ooh my, Robyn—all those blessèd *stairs* I have to climb. I don't think your father would like climbing them very much. It's too much for an old lady like me . . ."

Grandma had a point—she was over seventy and not a nimble figure. On some level, my father might have been getting his own back on her for her famous remark when she visited him in hospital after he was wounded:

"Well, I don't know I'm sure: I mean, who's going to want to dance with *you* now?"

The big house had outbuildings, too—quite a few of them. There was a creosoted garage with an abandoned office inside, still hung with green metal lampshades, though the lightbulbs were long unscrewed; the garage had a cement forecourt on which I fashioned primitive buses based on pram wheels. My sister and I sometimes wheeled the radio around there on Sundays as it blared *Pick of the Pops* out into the foliage. There were oil drums full of noxious jelly that we gradually cleared away. When I think of all that derelict junk now, I hear "You'll Never Walk Alone," sung by Gerry & the Pacemakers, bleeding out of that big radio as it sat in the pram like a tinny baby.

There were two fields, too, bordering on tangled forest that was common land. Nobody owned this overgrown zone beyond our fields; it never seemed to lead anywhere except back the way you came. It was rank with bracken and ponds, and should have been fun but wasn't. Yet if you looked closely, the undergrowth was crawling with worms, snails, stag beetles, frogs, and a black, scorpion-like insect with a segmented tail, the devil's coach horse.

Behind the shrubbery that grew outside my bedroom window there was a decrepit hut, full of sacks of flour, which was inhabited by two imaginary farmworkers who we named Bill and Fred. This was especially creepy at twilight, as was the coach house that stood next to the back entrance to the house. I would sit upstairs there, among the empty tins of rat poison and wisps of straw, filling up with fear until I was engulfed by it; then I'd scamper down the ladder, pursued by the demons I had conjured.

Did I like frightening myself? There wasn't much else to do. I had two male friends my age who both lived a couple miles away—occasionally one of them would cycle up the hill, past the hostile Alsatian dogs that guarded our neighbor's compounds, and join me digging tunnels. Sometimes I would go around to their houses and dig tunnels with them; tunnels that we could just about squirm along, elbowing our way through the damp earth past the severed roots of small shrubs. All three of us were oldest sons with two younger sisters, the postwar firstborn, digging tunnels. My father had been digging a trench in France in 1944 when the German shrapnel hit him.

There was a lot of space to play in, to dream things up. The dreams weren't always very comforting, but what is? My father was working off his nightmares, and I was working on mine. I often woke up at night discovering I had wet the bed. Eventually I learned to replace the soiled linen with fresh, climb into clean pajamas, and go back to sleep. Still, nightmares came easily in that house.

Around the time that I stopped wetting the bed, I

started, occasionally, smashing my things up. This was mid-1964, when "House of the Rising Sun" by the Animals was number one. I had made a balsa-wood tram, which I mounted on the chassis of a model train so it had rails to ride on. I had recently become an obsolete electric traction freak after my father gave me a bus-spotting book for my tenth birthday; this was perhaps his ironic comment on where my mother's money came from. So I made this handsome tram, and painted it black, white, and gray, the colors of an imaginary city corporation. I was very proud of it. It even won first prize in a "hobbies & crafts" competition at my school.

One overcast afternoon in July, out the back of the house behind the Parlor, I took a hammer and smashed that tram into slivers of nothing. Then I burst into tears and cried for several hours. I don't know where my parents were, but I got some comfort from our kindly Norwegian au pair, Randi. I didn't understand why I had smashed my tram—and I still don't: was it an experiment in making myself feel bad? If so, I succeeded. From time to time, for a few years after, if I became overwhelmed I would destroy something of mine that I valued—records usually. Nobody stopped me.

In the 1930s our house on the hill had been a diplomat's place, connected to the US embassy; allegedly Joseph Kennedy had once stayed there, when JFK and

Bobby were children. The servants who inhabited the attic would have sashayed down the back stairs when the bell rang to meet the needs of visiting guests. They probably served tea and cocktails on the terrace to visiting Americans as they stared across the Surrey landscape.

It had become a junkyard by the time my parents came across it. They did put a lot of effort and money into restoring it; at one point, they even installed two peacocks in a little shed. The plan was to keep the birds locked in there for two weeks, so their inner compasses would adjust themselves to this Surrey hilltop. However, Grandma was unaware of this plan; she let them out prematurely and they flew away.

"Ooh my, Robyn—those ruddy birds; I don't know *what* your father was thinking, keeping them in a cage like that. Anyway, nobody told me they had to stay in there."

Undeterred, my parents bought two more peacocks, which this time escaped by themselves. One of them wandered into the conservatory where we used to store wicker furniture so it could slowly get damp over the winter. My father chased the hefty bird as it flapped haplessly against the dusty glass panels:

"My God, the bloody animal is shitting all over the fucking chairs!" It upset him all the more to have so little agility. Twenty years with a stiff leg was taking its toll.

And he hated that we could all see him feeling vulnerable and inadequate.

"Well," said my mother, as my father subsided into his calmer self: "I think people might like some more tea; Robyn, darling, could you see if we have any chocolate biccies left?"

So the second pair of peacocks vanished too. The foxes ate at least one of them: my sister and I found some feathers and a stray foot outside the Bill and Fred hut. I saw the last of the giant birds roosting in a tree on the edge of the common, a few days later.

My parents also hired an Italian gardener who showed me how to shoot a piece of toast with an air rifle. He wore a beret.

The oddest feature of the place was the pigsties, which lay at the back of the property, behind the fields. They were a sort of Wild West village, two rows of dwellings facing each other. This place was a bonus for us children, the two of us who were old enough to walk, and for our occasional friends. The breeze-block buildings each had a room at the back and a kind of front garden. There were six or seven sties on each side of Main Street, and between them ran a concrete pathway. It was many years since pigs had had these buildings as a home address: by the time my sister and I colonized them, only one of the back rooms still had a roof. It was made of corrugated iron: no luxury for pigs. Elderflower saplings were thrusting up through the cement, and the seedlings that had taken root were gradually returning Pig Town to nature. In a few years, it would be totally overgrown, as any city will be if it's abandoned but doesn't flood.

What did we do down there, my sister and me and our occasional friends? We wheeled the radio in its pram, of course, and made small bonfires, on which my sister cooked stinging-nettle soup. If there were enough of us we played hide-and-seek. When it rained we took shelter under the one remaining pigsty roof; hearing the Beatles sing "From Me to You" still transports me back to that dark, musty pig boudoir. I kept a tin trunk of magazines in there, which I had buried for six months, and when I dug them up again they were moldy. I didn't know enough to wrap them in plastic to keep them dry. The magazines were full of black-and-white photographs of fairly naked women. They were somehow comforting. My father enjoyed them too.

It's April 1967, and my parents are about to leave the house and all its outbuildings to set up their next earthly paradise, just outside Winchester. I am down in the pigsties alone, with my own little radio. These days, even the BBC is playing more pop records.

The sun is shining. It shines down on the radio poised

on a breeze-block wall. I'm wearing a purple nylon shirt with a big collar. The sunlight is strong enough to cast thick black shadows across the ruined piggery. A clever new song comes on the air: "Say you'll be mine and I'll love you till Tuesday." It feels like the singer is trying too hard, but it catches my attention. "And that," says the DJ's voice, "was David Bowie."

Then something earth-shattering bursts out of the radio, albeit at ant volume. SKRONK-SKREEK-SKRONK-SKREEK: WHA-DA-DA-FANG, DA-DA-DA-FANG—"Purple Haze all in my brain / Lately things they don't seem the same"—Jimi Hendrix detonates Pig Town. The ghost porkers jive in the wasteland. Bill and Fred do the Watusi in their floury shed. My moldy magazines sprout fresh pages that turn themselves before my eyes. I am a teenager on fire—oh, holy fuck, this is music to levitate to . . .

Back in the haunted house, Grandma bakes an apple pie. My father paints a grotesque image of a shrieking fetus in a tin helmet. My mother smokes unfiltered cigarettes and reads an existential paperback. My main sister brews up a green potion. My little sister puts her doll Toots to bed, although it's only two in the afternoon. Jimi Hendrix plays a guitar solo such as my radio was never designed to reproduce. When it finishes I leave the pigsties forever.

It's still April, but now it's raining again so the English winter has resumed. Riding on the upper level of a bus to visit one of my designated friends, I read in the *New Musical Express* that the forthcoming Beatles LP has cost £13,000 to make so far; £13,000 is, as far as I can tell, the price of a whole street in Weybridge, Surrey, where three of the Beatles and I overlapped for a couple of years—not that I ever actually saw any of them. But I did dream that John Lennon in his Beatle boots collected me from school in a taxi. Anyway, their new LP is due to be released next month. The *NME* article is the first I've heard of it—and the first I've ever heard of a record costing money. Does that mean *Highway 61 Revisited* cost money to record too? I ask my mother about it.

"Well, things can be expensive, darling," she says in her natty silk headscarf, squinting toward some distant shrubs. The surviving peacock honks from within them.

Do Nothing until a Mistake Is Made

———

DOINNNNGGGG! It's late May and I'm back in the college. Jimi Hendrix has reached the House Gramophone. The groovers among my fellow inmates are trying to grow their hair long, out over their ears, over their collars, over their eyes, up toward the heavens—in every direction. There are mechanisms in place to thwart this tendency (that sentence is pure Winchester—every penny my parents paid of my fees went into writing it)—namely the housemasters:

"Hoh!" says Blotto, intercepting me sliding out of lunch one day. "I think a trim is called for here." I'm learning that the barber is the natural enemy of freedom. Soon I will learn the same thing about the police force.

The part of Winchester College where hair is at its most liberated is the original College itself, centered on the medieval courtyard—there the Scholars dwell. The College, of course, has the highest percentage of groovers; their parents, being academics and denizens of the mind in general, are less hung up on keeping their sons in short-back-and-sides than the dads and mums of inmates of the redbrick buildings such as Blotto's. I've started wandering into the Scholars' hive of late, where the sound of Jimi Hendrix is already fine-tuning the ambience via his Marshall amplifiers on shiny vinyl. Marshall stacks have yet to arrive in the Scholars' toad-kindling underworld, but they're on their way, just as they first reached me in ant form in the pigsties.

I walk into one of the Scholars' chambers. The sun shines through the cobwebs and dust in the windows. Although we're above ground, the spores of history below our feet are wafting up to enfold us. The room extends in many directions, past rafters and beams and bookcases laden with LPs and faded Faber poetry hardbacks. The customary varnished timber mixes with bare plaster, which makes the room feel both unfinished and long past its best. The Scholars potter from desk to fireplace, burning old manuscripts to keep warm. Emblazoned in toothpaste around the central arch that keeps the regency ceiling from crumbling onto the fourteenth-century floor is an adapted Jimi Hendrix quote:

THIS WALL WILL TURN BLUE TOMORROW
THIS WALL TURNED PINK YESTERDAY

The Scholars are self-aware enough to send themselves up even as they absorb a new fad: "Too much!" squeaks an omniscient figure in a black gown, waving his arms about. The Scholars all have to wear black gowns, in theory, but the advanced ones have learned the trick of making their gowns invisible. Incense caresses the air, while John Coltrane's saxophone plays from one speaker, and Hendrix's guitar from another.

"What's happening, man?" A group of Scholars have levitated and are sitting cross-legged below the ceiling: Galen, Simon, Jansch (who has renamed himself after Bert but is no relation), and the Ugly Pullover. Next to Bob Dylan, I feel like these people are most likely to know the meaning of life. They are a year or so older than me. I genuflect before them, in the damp straw:

"Hendrix is happening, my lieges—as ye may know. Across the plains and meads of Winchester, he . . ."

"Yeah, right, man," says the Ugly Pullover. "What are you doing on Sunday after chapel?"

"Er . . . I might see James Robertson Justice giving a lecture on tadpoles in Drainage Club, or . . ."

"No, man, you've gotta come here."

"Here? You mean to this precise spot?"

Up below the ceiling, they giggle, gently:

"Yeah—no, yeah, seriously, Robyn—there'll be an actual Happening, right below the floor."

"Er . . . below these very flagstones?" I try to nail things down as precisely as I can.

"Uh-huh, yeah: this floor you're standing on. It's Brian, you know?"

Then they float down to their positions around the fireplace, as if they'd been there all along. I so wish I had passed the Scholarship exam.

Next Sunday comes around, and back in Blotto's house after chapel I climb out of my straw hat and black suit, then don my jeans and newly acquired denim jacket. Should I wear my melon-pip beads, lovingly hand-threaded by my sister? No, I opt for a button-down orange shirt. I stomp back the way I have but lately come, through narrow streets and cloisters, past the chapel and into a small door across the courtyard from it. Down I slither into a cellar that's been there since 1382, a mere 585 years ago.

A few steep steps take my feet down to these ancient

flagstones. No sunlight has fallen on them for six centuries. I smell incense: a joss stick is taking the edge off the spores, and a blue lightbulb hanging from the ceiling gives the room a submarine tranquility.

The chamber itself isn't crowded. Twenty or so seats are ranged facing the master of ceremonies. To one side of them is a reel-to-reel tape recorder: its red light chimes with the glowing tip of the incense stick. Two wires run out of the tape machine: one leads to a microphone that is draped over the back of an empty chair. I sit down in the chair behind it, in the back row. The microphone dangles above my knees. The other wire leads to an electric violin, which is cradled by the Ugly Pullover.

The master of ceremonies is definitely a groover. I've seen him before around Winchester as he's at the local art school. He has thin shoulder-length hair and a pair of blue circular sunglasses. He's the logical extension of the Scholars; being slightly older than them, he has the aura of a sage. His name is Brian Eno and he seems to know something. Eno has the authority of a teacher, yet he's subversive like a rebel. I can't take my eyes off him, and nor can the other young inmates. I recognize Galen, and Simon, and Jansch: in fact, everyone in this underground chamber is a groover—there's not a meathead in sight. At the extreme left of the front row sits the hip young teacher, Mr. Felix—he's come along to keep an eye on us. Nobody is actually breaking any rules; none-theless the whole event feels transgressive. A telepathic murmur is underway.

Eno nods to the Ugly Pullover and the murmur fades. Then he strides across to the tape recorder and starts it up. Quietly it begins to play what I *think* is Bob Dylan singing "Ballad of Hollis Brown," backward. That voice is as hypnotic as ever, even in reverse. On cue, the Ugly Pullover starts running a bow over the open strings of the violin. It's a discord that mostly fights with the backward Dylan tape, but occasionally synchronizes with it.

The four elements are in place: blue lightbulb, incense, backward tape, and droning violin. The key to the event, however, is the reverence of the audience: the faith that we could not supply for the Church of England service in the chapel only an hour ago is conjured up in us and unleashed by Brian Eno. For fifteen minutes, or however long that reel of tape takes to unspool, we are absorbed by the Happening. We are witnessing a ceremony: it's uncertain what exactly the ceremony means, but Eno is definitely its high priest.

At one point, I tap the microphone, though no sound comes out of it. There are already two sonic narratives to compete with in this cellar. I look furtively around but nobody seems concerned so I lower my head and hum into the mic: again, nothing. I sit upright and resume what I imagine is a meditation posture. Part of me is most impressed to be involved in this event that has such a high groover content: I've obviously stumbled across something of enormous significance here. Part of me thinks it's a pretentious charade—probably the part of me that comes from the Forest of Dean.

"Any questions?" asks Brian, switching off the tape machine. The Ugly Pullover has lowered his violin and is sitting back down on a kitchen stool. The joss stick burns low.

Mr. Felix raises his hand:

"Yes, man?" says Brian.

"Well," says Mr. Felix, clearing his throat from the spore-and-incense fug that's beginning to coat it: "Er, how would you define this event: is this kind of thing still music—or is there a new term for it now?"

"Oh, it's all music, man: when you sneeze it's music, you know?"

Mr. Felix strokes his chin and nods his head politely. A few groovers titter at Eno's observation. He continues:

"But we must ask ourselves, do definitions help . . . or are they just another hang-up, you know?"

Mr. Felix looks at the floor and nods. Brian Eno looks around expectantly, awaiting the next contestant. Nobody else volunteers, so I put up my hand. Brian nods his blue sunglasses my way:

"Was that 'Ballad of Hollis Brown' on the tape you were playing?"

"Aha," replies the high priest, lowering his sunglasses briefly and twinkling his eyes in the dim light. "Would you like it to be? If you would, then it is . . ."

The groovers are delighted with this response and titter some more. Obstinately, I persist:

"What was this microphone for?"

"So you could do something in it, man: you know—participate."

"I tried but it was switched off."

"Next question?" says Eno firmly, looking at the other end of the audience . . .

I wonder, on my way back to Blotto's house, if witnessing this event is anything like getting stoned.

All the Lonely People:
Hodges and the Duplock

———

You may have noticed how much the world I'm describing is lopsided, gender-wise. The kindest word for it would be monastic. It's a culture where all people are male, and females are another species. Women exist mainly behind glass, like the *Mona Lisa* in the Louvre. We glimpse them through windows and in photographs, and though they may crowd our dreams and our memories, they aren't part of our daily life. There's people, and there's females.

So many of my fellow inmates have been at boarding school since the age of seven that the gender imbalance at the college doesn't seem that weird, to them. And of course, during the one-third of the year that you're home with your parents (back here in the mid-1960s divorce is rare, so they're usually still together), you are very likely to have a mother in the house, and a high likelihood of sisters too. I have two sisters, both younger than me but born into the same psychic landscape. Still, if the rest of your family has also been processed by boarding school, they too are likely to be monastic, at heart. So wealthy males and females are coupled for the purposes of reproduction, but otherwise lead separate lives as separate species under the same roof. One of the main functions of private education in Britain is to stunt people emotionally and then send them out to run the country.

However, the odd stray female can find herself inside a male colony such as Winchester College. One such person is Miss Nora Duplock, the house matron. I feel pity for her, and a slight revulsion too. Miss Duplock is a small woman marooned somewhere between sixty and seventy years of age. She has a square face, on which sit a little mouth and a tidy nose. A white net of hair clings obediently to her scalp. She wears a pink cardigan, a string of pearls, and an iron-gray pleated skirt. Flat, sensible shoes encase her feet; she has probably never worn high heels. To be fair, neither have most of our teachers, that we know of.

Miss Duplock (for who is there to call her Nora?) dwells alone in a suite of rooms somewhere on the western side of Blotto's house, just above the bike sheds. Her job is to minister to the sick: if you have the flu or a sprained ankle or any malfunction that doesn't involve your sex organs or the zone immediately around them, you go and see the Duplock, as we call her. If you become too unwell to attend classes there's a room with four beds in it, one of which you can lie in for a couple of days. It is Nora's task to feed you grapes and medication until you recover. For all intimate matters, there is a house doctor on call who will sort you out with mycosis creams, powders, and the like. Our colony is efficient: we have learned from the ants.

When she talks, Miss Duplock sounds wistful and occasionally peevish. She's resigned, lower-middle-class English; life has avoided her, mostly, but fate has washed her up at Winchester College. She could be a character in "Desolation Row," if she were better known. She's aware of her effect on people as she pads sadly, dutifully through the institution that now engulfs her: "No one comes near" is her mantra. When I first heard the Beatles sing "Eleanor Rigby" my thoughts flew to Nora Duplock: they seemed to be singing about her. She flits through the big house, a forlorn ghost long before her time of dying.

We inmates assume that she's always been unloved: a meal that nobody wanted to eat. In years to come, I'll look back and wonder if our contempt for the elderly virgin spinster was part of a greater misogyny that glazed our teenage eyes in that one-sex town. And one sex it is. As a teenage boy, your cock is your motor, and it can drive you to interesting and sometimes perilous places. In the absence of girls, and any real guidance from our embarrassed elders, we inmates have to experiment with ourselves, and with each other. Oddly enough, it's not until 1967 that homosexuality is legalized in the UK—odd because the men who oversee our legislation have been having sex with each other in our private schools for centuries. Whether they remain gay or not, members of the British ruling class largely start out that way.

Mostly, however, sex between adult humans is a matter of speculation for us inmates. How old, for example, can you be and continue to have sex: can elderly couples still manage it?

"Of course they can," says Gallows Junior with great authority. "There's nothing to stop them, is there?"

"Let us know when you get there, Gallows," leers Scraper from a bed across the way where he has just climaxed into a football sock. "Send us a postcard from the old folks' home."

"Yes," adds Martz: "Old people don't necessarily notice they're old—to them it's probably quite normal."

"Normal being old?"

"Well, old in a relative way—if you're both old, does either of you notice it?"

I'm not sure about this, having just witnessed my grandfather taking a piss in the bushes in the Forest of Dean. How can you fail to notice when you're urinating out of something that ancient? Stay alive and find out, son.

"Well, just imagine—I dunno," I cast my mind about here, "imagine Hodges fucking the Duplock."

This gets a laugh and a few groans from the assembled crowd.

"Hodges and the Duplock? That's disgusting," says Horse. "Hitchcock, why do you have to imagine such grotesque things all the time?"

Hodges is the master in charge of physical education. He has bushy ginger eyebrows that fly out at the sides like a pair of wings on his face. His voice is soft and singsong, with a hint of menace; oddly, it's like the voice of a radio disc jockey in some ways. That said, Hodges might sound out of place introducing the latest Jimi Hendrix Experience single over the airwaves on the BBC Light Programme:

"Now, here's a chap who's making his Uncle Hodges

very happy by putting in just a *little* extra time on the parallel bars every morning—it's Jimmy Hendricks and his Experiments with 'The Wine Cries Mary.'"

Hodges is another former Winchester inmate who has never undergone the full recovery and so finds himself back at the college again in later life. He has the arrested-development aura of a little boy fossilized in middle age, which makes him an unsettling presence. His nose strains forward like a cartoon gopher's and he sometimes wears a bow tie, when he's fully clothed.

Which he isn't always. Adjusting to life in the college, when you do eventually adjust to it, implants some patterns in your neurons that aren't easily uprooted. I know I've already mentioned this—that's patterns for you. Hodges is another like the Shoveler, the Dicker, the Bin, and the rest of them, who never achieved escape velocity. He's in charge of the gymnasium—it even has his drawings on the wall, showing miniature versions of himself with tiny wingèd eyebrows, exercising on each of the antique appliances (no machines: they're all varnished wood and coconut matting, natch). These tiny icons of Hodges swarm around the gymnasium walls like hieroglyphics in some lost wooden tomb.

At heart, in the way that some long-term rock 'n' rollers are, Hodges is a child. His clock stopped in his teens, and he is tethered to the college unless it ever starts again.

A quarter of a century later when I'm on a date with my future second ex-wife, we'll be sitting under an awning in the rain on a Winchester side street enjoying a cappuccino when a rickety old fellow is collected from the opposite pavement by two men in high-visibility jackets and gently placed in the back of a van. It's Hodges—the old boy on his final rounds in the Hampshire drizzle. So, it looks like he'll be cradled in an institution till the last. My future-ex nods politely when I put her in the picture, Hodges-wise.

Hodges will make it to the 1990s; back in 1967 he looks to be in his sixties, as does Nora Duplock. Biologically, yes, they could have sexual intercourse; though, not being married to each other, their tryst would scandalize the prim snow globe of Winchester College.

Who knows what they're really made of, inside? They would have both been adolescents during the First World War; conceivably, Nora as a girl might have had a young soldier sweetheart who was shipped off to France in the last year of the war, and never returned.

How would that have felt, to a teenager in love for the first time?

My darling Nora,
    How I long to see your sparkling eyes close up to mine; to feel your fingers intertwined with my own; to

brush your sweet rosy lips with my own stubbly mouth. O Nora, such sweet thoughts are torture to me in this ██████████, yet they are all that sustain me. To hold your little face again in my hands, these hands that have come into contact with—but why speak of the unspeakable? Without a glimpse of you at the end of this bleak tunnel, I would rather be ██████████ and ██████████.

How are you, my love? What is your world like this evening? We are scarcely 100 miles apart, yet might as well be on two separate planets. It's hard to believe, on the rare occasions that we see the sun through the drizzle, the smoke, and the gas, that this same sun is shining down on your sweet self a few degrees north as you walk over ██████████ Bridge in your adorable cape and nurse's cap.

Tomorrow my unit is due to ██████████ but who knows what will come to pass? Jerry has plans of his own, no doubt. For now all I have in my heart is you— yet that's enough. Not many of the fellows here are religious now, but I worship at the Church of Saint Nora the Divine, and my adoration of you, sweetheart, will see me to the shores of Heaven and beyond, I have no doubt. Your photograph is in a locket that I keep over my heart. If I ██████████ then Jerry will take us both, my love.

Write, please write, dearest Nora. Your last letter is

dog-eared and blurred from my fingers wishing I could somehow claw through the paper and find myself next to you again. I love you and I live for you.

Yours, always
Roy

Perhaps, nearly fifty years later, this letter is still in her desk. Too fragile now to turn over in her hands, it's held together in a cellophane envelope, through which Miss Duplock reads it every night before saying her prayers and climbing into her narrow bed. What does she pray for? What she's always prayed for, since a letter arrived one bright April morning in 1918 from Mrs. Fenwick, Roy's mother, bearing the awful, inevitable news . . .

And what of Miss Duplock's reply to her doomed beau? Was it among Captain Roy Fenwick's folded possessions when they eventually arrived back at the family home in Clapham, not long before the Armistice?

My Dearest Roy,

I am most grateful indeed to hear from you. Sister tells me so many others on our ward have heard little, or indeed nothing, from their sweethearts for some time now.

I blush to read your tender thoughts of us together; but you must not talk of me as one of the Saints—why,

Roy, that is blasphemy! Nonetheless I am very Touched by all you say. You are much better with words than me, Roy. It's awful to think of what you and the other brave Boys have to endure, all for our sakes. How can we ever show our gratitude, for we never can see you, any of you?

It has been cold here, but we make do. Sister brought some gammon to our Sunday dinner, and a couple of the nurses drank some beer, which they say made them quite giddy. I did not drink any beer, although perhaps I may try one glass with you when you return, Roy. Oh, to think of when you return: it makes me feel rather queer, even more lost for words. I so want you to return.

Mr. Ormrod has brought in a spaniel that his wife Hetty is looking after for the winter. It's a sweet little dog, and very considerate of Mr. Ormrod's way of walking that he's had since he returned. Perhaps you and I shall have a pup someday, Roy—if that is not too sinful a thought!

I'm due on duty shortly, so must sign off now to get the afternoon post.

With all my love,
Nora Duplock

Fifty years later, she has to look after a mob of boys not much younger than the boys who never came back from the Western Front.

Gunner's Hole and the Mail Balloons

———

Among the paperwork that my parents had to contend with when they consigned me to Winchester was one item absolving the college from any responsibility if I contracted Weil's disease. This is a rare sickness caught from coming into contact with infected rat's urine, and causes fever and nausea. The young inmates might find themselves catching this from bathing at Gunner's Hole, which was the school swimming pool. It's basically a stretch of river that is cordoned off into a rudimentary outdoor swimming area; the bottom of the pool is mud and the sides are concrete. Any number of unseen creatures might be crawling along below you or brushing your freezing limbs: you're swimming with the eels and the furry invisibles. Gunner's Hole, of course, has no heating and no chlorine to disinfect the water.

"Well," says Blotto, removing his pipe from his teeth and looking philosophically at some embossed wallpaper that has been catching pipe smoke since the 1920s: "I think you'd be very unlucky to actually catch Weil's disease—it's just a formality really."

"Gosh, sir, you can't even see into the water."

"Hoh! Well, my point exactly: who knows if the rats are even down there now?"

In the summer of 1967 Gunner's Hole is in its last days. In 1900 the *Public School Handbook* described it as "a high-diving erection with four stages and two springboards," and a high-diving erection it still is. As exercising zones go, the Hole is adequate: once you've surrendered yourself to the dark waters, you can swim up and down all you want, pretending to be a giant water rat or perhaps a beaver. The River Itchen, which feeds our swimming area, is one of the clearest streams in Britain. Things aren't quite so clear in the Hole, however. Still, most swimming in Britain when I'm growing up is out of doors: in icy-blue lidos or cold pebbly seas. Like so much in life, it's sustained by tradition: the past is a spine that leads you to the present.

One sunny afternoon, I'm at Gunner's Hole standing outside the thatched huts that function as changing rooms. I've just swum and am wrapping myself in one of the threadbare college-issue towels, patting down my goose bumps. It's June and the sun is fairly high. I'm aware of somebody standing near me, who I think is a Scholar: they're not so easy to identify without their black gowns.

"Ah," sighs the Scholar, who is also wrapped in a towel, "you know they used to bathe naked here, didn't they?"

"Er, did they?"

"Oh yes," continues my companion, wistfully: "I rather miss those days, don't you?"

Before I can reply, a voice shrieks behind us:

"Gangway!"

It's Hodges, stripped to the onions: it's as if he's stepped out of the Scholar's mind. He comes charging from the changing room, naked—his nose and his cock aligned in a directional way toward the dark river that awaits him. His russet eyebrows and his gingery pubic hair show how much iron must be in his system; if you left him out in the rain too long he might rust. His eyes seem to be shut, and he sprints with arms and hands stretched out before him, like a sleepwalker's. Is he, in fact, asleep? I can't reflect on this because Hodges is flying like a jet fighter over a hedge—his stocky, ferric body splashes into the water in half a second, bursting the surface and sending ripples all the way to the opposite bank. He seems even more of a cartoon character without his clothes. True to his early programming, he likes to swim naked at Gunner's Hole. Just as the Shoveler likes to shower with the boys in his charge. Both of them are former inmates, of course. They want that naked young feeling, one more time. And again . . . and again.

A few thickets and streams away lies a large flat green field, surrounded by chestnut and plane trees. It seems manicured, and it is: it's the main college cricket ground. This is the most picturesque part of the school. Low-lying buildings crouch at the edge of the pitch: the science school ("Stinks Block" in Notions-speak), the cricket pavilion, and a dark wooden hut known as Oily Hatch. When the Hatch is lifted on summer afternoons, it opens onto a counter where you can buy confectionery and soft drinks: Bounty coconut bars, Crunchie bars, Cadbury's Flakes, Fry's Turkish Delight; ice creams in cones and wafers; Coke tins and bottles of sweet, fizzy, colored water: these are here to give you a sugar buzz that will keep you coasting through the meager school rations.

This inspires an early poem of mine:

Gem for Nora and Everybody Else
If you look at your reflection in a Coke tin
You will notice that you are yellow and bent:
This probably just about sums you up

I am beyond thrilled when this eventually makes it into the school magazine.

Beyond the cricket pitch lie the water meadows, and beyond them rises St. Catherine's Hill. Given the gruesome end St. Catherine met, it's quaint that this Neolithic swelling in the Itchen Valley is named after her. Long before her time, before the church of Jesus reached the British Isles, the hilltop was an Iron Age encampment: somewhere between a fortress and a chapel, with an exhilarating outlook across the valley. Here the Druids might have kept watch for UFOs in prehistoric times.

A short interval: the signal from 1967, it wavers. It's not always a steady beam transmitting. It's soothing to tune in to it from fifty-five years later—fifty-six now, in fact— but sometimes it's faint. Occasionally I have to search around for a familiar image on which to center the narrative . . .

Right about this point in 1967 my young skeleton must have reached its present length. The first traces of mustache are about to appear above my top lip—it's the dawn of body hair. My cock is in a nest of dark wires and needs to discharge itself frequently. Looking back from the other end of life I feel amazed and a tad envious: who the fuck was I, this teenage creature? I'm in this narrative from a time so remote that it might as well be a historical novel. Best get on with it, Hitchcock . . .

It's Sunday again, and it's sunny. Brian Eno is staging another Happening, this time outside the Science Block, not far from Oily Hatch. Everybody casts a strong black shadow on the grass below them. There are cylinders of helium being wheeled around by a man in a white coat, his high-domed forehead and spectacles glinting in the sunlight. He is Captain Physics, one of the science teachers. The sun also reflects from the round blue sunglasses of Brian Eno. His hair, too, is already in retreat on his still-teenage head, but it's straggling down to his shoulders, enhancing his sage aura. He stands among the Scholars, who have had a refreshing night's sleep hanging upside down from the rafters and are ready for action, after the obligatory bath of Christianity from the Sunday chapel service.

Since Eno's event in the cellar the month before, life has

moved on. Up in Gloucestershire our granny has died. All around the world, the Beatles's *Sgt. Pepper's Lonely Hearts Club Band* has been released: groovers, meatheads, straights, and swingers—even the military—everybody has a copy. I wonder what Granny would have made of it.

Today's Happening is music free. It involves writing messages on small cardboard labels and then tying each one to a balloon that Captain Physics has filled with helium from a nozzle attached to a gas canister. He hands the balloons to Scholars and other senior groovers, who in turn hand them to us.

I get a brief audience with Eno himself:

"What are the balloons for . . ." I almost call him "sir" but remember the correct form of address just in time, ". . . man?"

Eno grants me the knowing glance of the true enigma:

"Well, they're not really *for* anything, man; thinking that everything has a purpose is a hang-up, you know?"

"Oh, right." I nod my head; message received and understood.

"But these balloons are like postcards, you know? Postcards to infinity . . ."

A couple of the Scholars giggle knowingly. Could they possibly be stoned? I wonder. I mean, what are the signs—how would I know? These guys always seem to know something I don't: they can see further into things than I can.

The balloons are larger than the usual party ones I've grown up with; pumped full of helium they wobble up into the air like fat silver teardrops. This morning the sky is a saturated blue, just right for a silver balloon. Eno's observation about postcards has given me an idea. When I get to the front of the short queue, a Scholar hands me a small brown cardboard label and a marker. I take the lid off and sniff the black tip: I love to inhale the acetate. Then I write a short card to my newly departed grandmother:

Dear Granny
   I'm sorry I couldn't go to your funeral.

Love,
Robyn

The Scholar reads it as he attaches it to a freshly inflated balloon handed to him by Captain Physics.

"Oh, that's beautiful, man . . . I'm sure your granny will be very touched." He hands me the balloon, gently: "Do you want to . . . do the honors?"

I take the balloon by its little umbilical tube with my card now flapping from it. The balloon obviously wants to escape and join its comrades, so I raise my arms up and let it fly away. My message to Granny soars away over the Winchester rooftops.

* * *

Back in the G House hive dining hall, Blotto is serving up the lunch. There are roast potatoes, it being Sunday. Blotto is looking dapper in a dark suit and waistcoat:

"Hoh! Any more for any more? Gallows, you're looking peckish . . . care for a few more potatoes?"

"Oh, I'd better not, sir—we've got rowing practice after lunch."

"Ah, of course—jolly good. And you, Hitchcock, what are you up to?"

Sunday afternoons are Free Time: you can do anything you want, as long as it's permitted.

"Oh, well, sir"—I manage to avoid addressing Blotto as "man"—"I think I'll go to the Art Room. Actually, I wouldn't say no to another roast—"

"Ah, of course: the Muse beckons. Hoh! I might have known . . ."

I glance around the other tables. Nora Duplock sits at the head of one of them, joylessly toying with her beef. She doesn't look like she's going to get very far with her roast potatoes either. Her pink cardigan can warn people off for miles. Next to her sit a few luckless inmates who haven't managed to find anywhere else. Only the dutiful Gollygosh attempts to make polite conversation with the sad old lady.

"Ah well, Miss Duplock—it's a lovely afternoon."

"Oh, yes . . ." The veil of despair over Nora's eyes hardens to a kind of malice: "I suppose it is."

"Are you going to go for a walk?"

"Oh no, I can't possibly go anywhere. I've been waiting for some pillowcases but . . . no one comes near." With a napkin folded tightly square, she pats the mouth in her square little face. What is it about suffering that drives other people away?

Gollygosh grunts politely and tackles his remaining potato. The Art Room it is . . .

The Art Room is several rooms, up a marble staircase in another chilly Victorian building. It is populated by stone statues, busts, and plinths from the nineteenth century, all in a dead ivory sheen. The building is in fact called Museum and it is exactly that. Occasionally lectures are given here on some aesthetic element of antiquity, but basically what lives here is a fossilized eroticism; the place screams sex. But rather in the same way that a human skeleton whispers love.

The Art master is a short, bald gay man with a snub nose and glasses; it's his misfortune, as an aesthete, to have to be the main model for the forty or so inmates who are taking Art as an A level and have to do a certain amount of drawing from life. So, hundreds of unflattering sketches of him cover the white walls that stretch up to the glass skylights. He gazes back at himself, nostrils and all.

Perhaps that constant reminder of the gap between the ideal and reality of his own existence is what makes him a sympathetic man. He has a private income to supplement his wages from teaching, no wife, and who knows how many friends he can number among the staff at the college? He also has a housekeeper named Mrs. V who makes exquisite sandwiches. In an underfed world such as ours, these sandwiches are currency.

The primary sandwich in Britain in 1967 is still cheese and tomato, closely followed by ham (sometimes with mustard) and chicken; a runner-up is egg and cress. I suspect Eno would probably prefer a hybrid, like ham and cress, though I never ask him. These archetypes can be dry and curling or, occasionally, succulent and moist—not unlike weather conditions.

Mrs. V's sandwiches are something else; it's hard to tell even what's in them. I think there are sardines in some, and maybe beef or shrimp—they're cut from soft brown bread from which Mrs. V trims the crusts, and their interiors are laced with some kind of mayonnaise. They pretty much eat themselves. I can inhale half a dozen of them washed down with some actual leaf tea from a porcelain teapot, but still stagger back to Blotto's house for beans on toast. We all of us are growing boys.

Lusting after the food prepared by private chefs for tables of the wealthy is very much Bertie Wooster territory, but Wooster and his fellow posh oafs would never have made it into the college: they (unlike their author, P.G. Wodehouse) were too dumb. We Winchester "Men," as we are called, like to believe we are smarter than that. If that sounds arrogant, that's partly what our parents are paying for: so that we become wise old men at seventeen. We are learning to know about everything without actually experiencing it.

But we sometimes learn that everything comes at a price. The Art master has customized his little terraced house in the backstreets of Winchester; he's got the means to make certain modifications that the other teachers probably wouldn't make even if they could afford to. His back garden is paved but thronged with bamboo and exotic plants so high and thick that the walls around aren't visible: you could be in a jungle. The garden area backs into a greenhouse where tropical growths blossom—I've never seen them before: nobody seems to know what they're called. And in the middle of the greenhouse is a microscopic swimming pool. It's square and white-tiled; unlike Gunner's Hole, you can see to the bottom of it.

"Come on, boys—let's have a swim, shall we?"

Slowly, incredulously, the five or six inmates who have been invited to fill themselves with Mrs. V's sandwiches strip off their clothes and fall or clamber into the pool, naked. The Art master does the same. He removes his glasses and without them he's more difficult to distinguish from the other pink, thrashing forms. The water is warm and chlorinated—it would probably be pleasant to wallow in there by yourself, or with a chosen companion. Thankfully the Art master does not become aroused; nor does anybody else. The scene is just too weird, and embarrassing. So nobody mentions it, on the whole. Are Blotto or the other housemasters aware of this potential orgy site in their gray-flint midst? They must be, but nobody says anything. Don't ask, don't tell.

The nude-bathing event only happens once for me. Maybe there are repeats for those who are more into it. The sandwiches are delicious, though: Eno doesn't know what he's missing.

Back in G House, Blotto has banned us inmates from burning incense:

"Hoh! Conducive to drugs: I think not. No more of them."

"But, sir—the other houses can burn them—it's not fair."

"Well, that may change. Anyway, I'm not letting you lot burn them."

This is what is becoming known as a bummer. Lighting up a joss stick and playing Dylan's "Sad Eyed Lady of the Lowlands" is a favorite ritual of Martz and mine and our semi-groover circle. But Blotto has a point, even if the idea that burning incense will turn us into dope fiends is a tad paranoid; the thick, smoky scent is pretty good at camouflaging tobacco. Though it would take a lot to camouflage the smell of Blotto's pipe.

Redux: Naked Teachers 2, Incense 0.

At 45 rpm in the Desert

———

When the school term ends in July 1967, my family doesn't actually have anywhere to live, so we stay for a month at Granny's up near the Forest of Dean while our new home is being finished. As Granny herself has just died, however, the atmosphere is a little skewed.

When my grandfather looks in the bathroom mirror, he can still hear his late wife's voice in his head: "Arthur, have you taken your teeth out yet?"

My mother is upset by her mother's passing but tries not to show it, and I pretend not to notice. Feelings are embarrassing, darling. I make a balsa-wood coffin for Toots, my youngest sister's doll. She is quizzical about this. My main sister becomes furiously creative, turning candle wax and melon pips into beads with which she thoughtfully supplies me. The melon-pip ones work best for me as they don't melt. I never realize how lucky I am to receive things.

But I have my guitar, and one of my cousins, bless him, lends me a life-changing item: a battery-operated gramophone. This has been a fruitful season for records, including some classic 45s. The Kinks's "Waterloo Sunset" and "A Whiter Shade of Pale" by Procol Harum have both landed on the turntable at school and are in heavy rotation. The cloudy summer twilights imprint themselves forever in my mind as those songs take up permanent residence in my head. Both have a dramatic melancholy about them, looking out at life through a prism where time has briefly stopped. Like *Sgt. Pepper*, which has also followed me up to the Forest, they already sound as if they've been around forever.

There's one 45 in the selection that my cousin kindly supplies me with that is new to me, by a group named Pink Floyd. It's called "Arnold Layne" and feels very direct: it tells in an ominous flat English voice of a man who steals clothes from a washing line in the moonlight; eventually he is arrested for this and banged up in jail. The voice seems to relish this harsh tale, and the music is punctuated by sound effects. There's nothing timeless or dreamy about this record: it's urgent and demented, in a compelling way. The singer sounds like he fancies himself a little; I'm not sure about him. There's a reference to "Baby Blue" in there, so they obviously know Bob Dylan. I'm intrigued.

On the record label I read that the composer's name is Syd Barrett: his first name is artfully misspelled, like mine is. The record was produced by one Joe Boyd. That's a more ordinary name, though it too contains the letter Y. The B-side is also written by Barrett and produced by Boyd: it's called "Candy and a Currant Bun." The voice seems too English to be using Americanisms like "candy," but I suppose the British term "sweets" wouldn't scan; nor would the grander "confectionery." This song has more sound effects on it, and a guitar solo that really sticks in my head.

Up in the Desert—my new post-Granny term for my mother's homeland—I keep the guitar and the record player under the bed. They're a shrine that I sleep above. So one day I haul out the guitar, fish up the record player, drop the needle on "Candy and a Currant Bun," and play along. It's the bottom string, the thickest one, that the Pink Floyd guitarist seems to be playing. Although I haven't worked out how to tune the string yet, it sounds fairly like the guitar on the record: BOW—WUMP—BOWWW— WUMP—BOWWW—WUMP, DONG! BOW— WUMP—BOW—WUMP—BOWWW—WADDLER WADDLER, WADDLER WADDLER, WADDLER WADDLER, WADDLER WADDLER—SPAT!

After a couple of days I can play it more or less correctly. The tune of the song sounds like it's based on "Smokestack Lightning" by Howlin' Wolf—but the guitar solo is something else: and now I can just about play it—yaysville!

Nineteen sixty-seven is the year of the guitar virtuoso, among other things. Clapton and Hendrix enter our
vocabulary like cheese and chocolate; only squares like
Blotto, Gollygosh, and the Duplock are immune to their
magic. But—maybe because I'm not drawn to being a
virtuoso (or there's nobody around to instruct me in
note-bending)—I'm not drawn to mimic them. But this
guy playing the guitar solo on the bottom string . . . Syd
Barrett? I can identify with him.

And the name Joe Boyd spins around and around on
the record label. I picture him as a very knowing fellow
in blue jeans and leather jacket. I figure that, like the
groovers in college, record producers must know something—they must have some insight to be involved in
these sacred pieces of plastic that have become the grails
of our lives.

Earthly Paradise, Take 2

———

"Childhood is the only totalitarian state, darling," my mother sometimes murmurs to me as she lights up a Player's Navy Cut cigarette. She lives in newspapers and paperbacks—she's more comfortable watching than participating, I think. That summer she gets me reading William Faulkner and Virginia Woolf; I'm not sure I fully understand their writing but I'm grateful for her input. Both of my parents love words: my mother loves reading them, my father loves writing them.

Part of this totalitarian state is moving house, into places that require ever-increasing renovation. The creepy house on the hill where our family lived when this narrative began had taken us a whole year to make habitable, even while we were living in it. In August 1967, after months adrift, my family finally moves into a converted water mill in Hampshire—only three miles from Winchester itself—which my parents have been having renovated for eighteen months. It smells of carpentry, being almost entirely a new building constructed inside a gutted exterior. It's an optimistic aroma.

The air is clear, the grass by the roadside has reached its height and is beginning to die back. Autumn waits offstage while the Summer of Love pirouettes through its finale, and momentum roars on for a little longer. But Brian Epstein is about to die, and unbeknownst to me, Syd Barrett is already alienating himself from the rest of Pink Floyd with his inexplicable mood swings; and where in the universe is Bob Dylan, the man who started it all? He's only been on my map for eighteen months, but I can trace so much in music back to him: Jimi Hendrix, David Bowie, Pink Floyd, and the way the pop groups now use words—it's all his doing. And he's vanished: if he's still alive even, what can he be up to?

It's pretty clear to me that Dylan knows the meaning of life, if anybody does. He has momentum, direction, intuition—wisdom. My elders and betters—teachers and parents, people who drive cars and look compromised— they have experience and they call the shots: they decide where you live and where you go, and until recently they told you when to go to bed, too. But they haven't seen to the bottom of the barrel the way Dylan has: they haven't glimpsed the fundamental pointlessness of everything.

Or if they have, they can't acknowledge it. Bob Dylan appears to have accessed (or created?) a world outside morality, faith, rules, or superstition: he's found the sad, doomed kingdom where things simply are—for no apparent purpose—and whose denizens haplessly await their fate. There's nothing they can do about it but breathe and wait for eternity.

I don't realize it yet, but that surreal awareness is where compassion of a kind can grow. T. S. Eliot may have got there first, in writing *The Waste Land*, but he couldn't sing it. Dylan adds the gift of incantation to his insight. Maybe it's too much to ask, for my parents to pay the Second World War veteran teachers of Winchester College to teach us about futility. And these smart veterans all wear ties: I've never seen Bob Dylan in one. Though I've never seen a photo of T. S. Eliot without one.

One afternoon in late August I stomp through the high grass just over the gate that opens onto the bridge across the clear river that my parents' new house bestrides. It's become a 1960s update of a medieval mill house, where flour was ground and trout were fished from the rippling water. If you stand still on the riverbank you can often see these fish hovering above the green strands of waterweed, swimming to stay motionless. The mill is redbrick in a tasteful, pre-loved way, with a score of modern single-pane windows that reflect the river valley like a row of square eyes.

Inside the house, the bedrooms are small: tiny cabins that focus the three of us, my sisters and me, on our desks. Compact bunk beds are built into the walls of golden varnished wood. I pin a Bob Dylan poster up on my wall immediately.

The three cabins and a small guest room are off a corridor looking west across to the bridge with its three low-lying arches, which specialize in reflecting the sunset in the water. Above the bridge lean spindly trees that etch their silhouettes against the pink and orange dusk. To me this echoes the dayglo sundowns that are beginning to appear on psychedelic posters.

The river flows under the bridge from beneath the north end of our house, where the mill wheel once was. Directly above it, the corridor of which I was writing a few sentences ago (but that was awhile back) leads over a short, elevated bridge to my father's new studio, upstairs from the former cowshed, which is right next door. This former cowshed is his mother's new residence. At least Grandma doesn't have to climb a flight of Victorian stairs anymore to get into it.

"Ooh my, Robyn—I'm at ground level once more. I suppose I should be grateful your father didn't stick me up in the attic again."

I know better than to try to play this grandmother any Dylan records. She likes old songs from the 1920s. She sits in front of her television singing along to them when the old-time shows come on. Her voice is strong and her pitching is good. Neither of my parents can sing—they lack the confidence, perhaps, or they are too aware of themselves. Grandma is a large and in a way handsome woman, another who is still suffering the consequences of the Great War. A gentle bitterness suffuses her: like Nora Duplock, she's a castaway. The currents of life, steered as they are by men, have beached her in the house of her only son. She and he are not close, though he forces himself to have coffee with her every morning, sitting there with his stiff leg and his brain full of art and longing. Grandma bores him with her litany of trivia: letters she has to post and pies she has to bake.

Her art is making pastries: she measures out her life in apple pies. She understands the alchemy of flour, eggs, and butter as she shuffles around her kitchen table, neatly conjuring the succulent pastry into being with her puffy fingers and a dainty butter knife. But she cannot share the joy of this with her damaged son.

She married a young army captain named Jack in 1915. Jack went to war in France and was wounded, though not severely:

"When he came back he was never the same again, Robyn."

"How had he changed, Grandma?"

"It was like I didn't know him anymore, really. Perhaps I never did . . ."

Grandma and I get along quite well, as often happens with grandparents and grandchildren—they can both take comfort in each other, ganging up on the generation in the middle. She shakes her head:

"Jack was a loner, Robyn: he should never have married. Preferred his own company, he did. I didn't see him for five years when he went to Palestine . . ."

After the Great War, Jack remained in the army, taking administrative posts around the British Empire. Grandma gave birth to my father in India. It was hot out there, far too hot to be having a baby. My father remained an only child, as Jack had been. Distance was the key, as it so often is in British families.

"If we were on a train with Jack, he would travel in one compartment and we would be in another one. Officers didn't ride with their wives . . ."

If Grandma measures out her life in pies, she punctuates it with sayings:

"They say it's the Devil's blackberries in October, Robyn: you don't want to pick them then."

"They say if snow lies around on the ground, it's waiting for fresh snow to join it."

"Your grandfather got the OBE—you know what they say that's for?" Lowers voice. "Other Bugger's Efforts."

She didn't relish her time in India, but some version of a local dialect entered her vocabulary and has stayed there:

"You're puggle you are, Robyn, ooh my."

"Ooh my, look at you: you need to do a pani."

Her hair is swept back up almost like a quiff, rinsed lightly and tinted with blue or purple dye. She is always in skirts: ladies of her generation never wear trousers. She walks up the hill to the bus stop once a week to get the bus into downtown Winchester.

I walk up the hill too, and wonder if I am a child or an adult. My feet are quite large now, encased in sneakers at the end of blue-and-gray-striped trousers. My sneakers scuff the potholes in the tarmac as I stomp up to the bus stop. Like Grandma, I'm going into Winchester, but for no apparent reason. I don't know anyone who lives here, once all the college has gone home. I'm not adult enough to look for Brian Eno—will I ever be? It's weird being in the town during the holidays—it's now my home patch but I don't know anyone in it, nor do I know how I'd meet them. My private-schooled personality is already starting to disqualify me from simply hanging out and meeting people. Perhaps it always had, but now I'm becoming aware of it. I'm over six feet tall, with a Beatle haircut and a caterpillar monobrow above my dark eyes. I'm starting to look inward, partly because I have no friends of my own age to look out at. Or with.

My father is beginning to come out in me. Perhaps he gave us children our three little cabins to help shoehorn us into our own worlds. My life becomes about art: I draw, I write, I play the guitar. Like him, I can exist largely in the confines of one room. "I am becoming an introvert," I write in one of my notebooks. It's the first time I use that word—I've never used it before—but it's accurate.

"You're becoming self-obsessed," observes my father, who can relate best to other people in terms of himself: "You're like me, Robyn, you're a solipsist," or, "You're not like me, Robyn, you like to see people." I've never felt very comfortable with him, perhaps because he's never felt very comfortable with me, or with himself. But slowly he is mutating into a kind of older brother, a role that fits him better than being a dad. I hear what he says and I absorb it.

Now that I'm eighteen months into boarding school and sprouting into puberty, my mother feels farther away. I am less inclined to share my thoughts with her. She can probably sense this, but, being the cagey soul she is, she wouldn't want to confront me about it. My main sister is still on the child side of adolescence, while I'm undergoing the change, so we aren't on quite the same frequency as before. My youngest sister is now five, with a black and white op-art dress. She has a new doll called Inch. All of us are moving through time.

I wish I had a girlfriend. I wish I had a friend, really. I'm a teenager and I'll stay one for the rest of my life.

The 5000 Spirits or the Fish on the Hill

What I lack in human friends I more than make up for in fish. The river is full of them. It flows directly under the house, so my father has had the idea of diverting some of it into a water tank in the entrance hall. There is therefore a pit of dark water in an area where there might normally be floor. It is set away from the front door (which is at the side of the house) so people are less likely to fall into it. The indoor water quickly develops a muddy silt bed of its own, as the river water slowly flows in and out of it. My father has had fun with Brian the architect in rebuilding this place: his large studio, his mother in the cowshed below him, us three kids in our little cabins, our mother with no actual room of her own other than the marital bedroom—does this show his priorities, perhaps? To be fair, he does work at home, and my mother doesn't officially need a job. He is in fact writing a novel (his painting phase is over now). *(This will earn him a great deal of money when he sells the film rights. But that is a step into the future beyond 1967.)*

The indoor water pit seems like a perfect home for water creatures, so I get hold of a net and bucket and start stalking the river for whatever swims or crawls through it. I don't have the patience to actually set up a rod and line and fish properly—that's for the adults. But when I trawl through the muddy riverbed, my net occasionally scoops out freshwater crustaceans known as crayfish. They're bulbous, armor-plated creatures about three inches in length that keep to themselves, crawling through the silt at the bottom of the river in total darkness. They have prominent front claws and countless legs pulling them along. Their nose tapers down to a conical point: this is where I imagine the pilot and copilot would sit if they were an aircraft. They're too small for humans to eat, unlike their luckless seaborne cousin, the lobster, so these crayfish lead a quiet life, on the whole.

As a hunting giant, however, I have other plans for them. When I tire of playing along to my records or designing my own psychedelic posters, I throw my full focus at the river, scooping my net through the bright green weed waving in it like underwater hair. Sometimes I haul up silvery little minnows, with a pulse flickering below their flat round eyes. Occasionally I find a fat, triangular fish writhing in the net:

"That's a miller's thumb," says Len, the stocky, stubbly water bailiff who patrols the riverbank. "Those are predators."

"What's a predator, Len?"

"Ha! 'What's a predator?' You should know that with your expensive education and all."

Len bristles—you could strike a match on him. I am soft and embarrassed:

"Er, no, sorry, Len—we haven't done that word yet."

"Ah, now, a predator is summat that preys on other creatures, like. So a predator fish eats other fish, see? Like this miller's thumb here."

Len is gratified to be broadening my education. His son Chris attends the local state school and speaks in a high, Hampshire accent; at fourteen I'm already beginning to sound like a BBC newscaster.

I take everything I catch back into the house in my bucket: minnows, miller's thumbs, a couple of crayfish, and one elderly trout that I nabbed as it hovered just under the bridge—I tip all these creatures into the dark water tank. When I look later, all the fish have vanished; either they've exited down the pipe that pokes up in the water like a periscope—or perhaps the miller's thumbs have eaten them, then eaten each other? But late that night when I come downstairs and switch on a light that is strategically angled into the tank, I see a solitary crayfish edging along the concrete bottom of the tank, wondering what happened to the riverbed.

* * *

It's the equinox and time to return to the college, which is now only three miles away from where I live: I could walk there in under an hour. Although I resent having to revert to wearing a twee straw hat and jacket and tie to wander through my new hometown of Winchester—now it's term time again—I'm actually happier at school, because I have friends there. Well, people who I know, anyway . . .

I arrive in G House with a jar of river water containing three minnows and a strand of waterweed, which I place on the desk in my cubicle in the Hall. Unlike the other boys, I never upgrade my cubicle to one of the bigger ones as I go up the ladder of seniority—I just stay where I initially landed. It's my home now. But when I come down for cornflakes the next morning, the three fish are curled lifelessly in the water.

The face of Horse appears over the curtain behind which I'm sitting with my dead fish:

"If you ever pulled your head out from the gramophone for half an hour, Hitchcock, you'd realize that fish need oxygenated water to breathe in."

"Well they were okay yesterday," I reply, shaking my head.

"Next time you want to swim in a jar, Hitchcock, make sure it's full of bubbles."

I never mean to kill the creatures I catch, but I'm not good at keeping them alive.

That afternoon I'm leafing through the LPs in the local record shop when my fourteen-year-old fingers find an LP sleeve of the most brilliant colors. I ease it from the rack and trace the lettering on the multicolored mountain range on the front: THE INCREDIBLE STRING BAND spells itself out in jagged candy stripes, beneath an all-seeing eye that peers from below a female/male figure who is caught midway between day and night. Of course: the Incredible String Band!

I've been listening to their first album that summer, along with my LPs by their fellow Scotsmen Bert Jansch and Donovan.

The cover alone of this new record, *The 5000 Spirits or the Layers of the Onion*, sums up everything I love about how 1967 is going so far. The saturated joy of it, the intricacy: everything seems to be turning into something else when you look at it closely; which, for me, is what defines psychedelia. My heart pulses like a minnow.

I buy the record without hearing a note, whisk it back to my lair at school, and pour it onto my record player. My parents have given me some money for helping to clear up the house on the hill, which they ended up selling at a profit: with that I've bought a portable record player of my own, like the one my cousin loaned me. It folds neatly into a maroon plastic case and is now my constant companion.

I drop the needle on "Chinese White" and am immediately transported to Incredible String Land. The music is like the cover: teeming with joy and a mysterious darkness that underpins it. The songs are simultaneously celebrations and laments; like Dylan, Mike Heron and Robin Williamson seem to sense how sadness is the shadow of beauty. Unlike Dylan, they also sense the holiness of all living matter. These people must be very stoned. I don't yet know what exactly it is to be stoned, and I know probably it may not be the answer, but it will surely help me ask the right questions—won't it?

On the back cover, amid rays of streaming color, Mike and Robin are photographed in a nook of vegetation, staring profoundly into the ivy. I have always liked hiding in bushes, and I make a mental note to continue to do so. Also on the album credits—and the Elektra label on the record itself—the name Joe Boyd reappears as producer. Whoever Joe Boyd is, he has to be a high-level groover. I add Heron and Williamson to Dylan as names of people who probably know the meaning of life, and I play *The 5000 Spirits or the Layers of the Onion* at least once a day in any local nook I can find around the college, or on the House Gramophone.

"Wow, Hitchcock," remarks Mudfellow, striding into Hall in his football gear: "Why have we only been treated to the Incredible String Band once today?"

"Oh, I can play it again if you like," I reply in all innocence. "I didn't want to overdo it."

"Oh, please don't bother on my account," is the riposte, as Mudfellow strides off to have a shower.

Music snob wars abound. On the House Gramophone somebody (Horse?) has written, "INCREDIBLE? STRING BAND."

Horse is playing "Daydream Believer" by the Monkees. I've enjoyed watching the *Monkees* TV show at home on our black-and-white television, but it's filtered through to me that they aren't hip: they are teenybopper pop, fodder for the meatheads.

"Oh come on, Hitchcock—let yourself enjoy it. You know it's good, even if it's by the Monkees."

"Yeah, but . . ." I'm at a loss for words. "I mean . . . they're not cool, are they?"

"Oh, for Chrissake!" Horse laughs at me like an old man in a pub might. "Music doesn't have to be cool to be good, does it?"

He has a point; and "Daydream Believer" is a very catchy song, like all the material the Monkees cover. That's part of the problem for me: if you don't write your own songs, you're not authentic. You're not saying anything of your own, you're merely singing words that someone else has put in your mouth. So Elvis Presley and Frank Sinatra, they're just supper-club singers—music for uncles. And the Monkees, to an earnest groover of 1967, are in that category too.

So I can't let myself enjoy them too much . . .

At the beginning of the summer and autumn terms, another bizarre ritual is enacted at Winchester College. The entire school and teaching staff rise at 7 a.m. and walk from their various hives up to the top of St. Catherine's Hill. They follow an ancient trail through the water meadows, past the sewage processing plant, under the viaduct for a now-abandoned railway line, and up a narrow ravine beneath a tiny bridge known as Kate's Cunt, which leads steeply up to the summit of the Hill. There's a ring of trees up there, and all the atmosphere of a Neolithic site, without any giant stones or a burial mound. To the south of the trees there is a clear area of grass and bracken, just large enough to accommodate the five hundred or so young inmates and their overseers.

When the whole troop is assembled, a senior Scholar musters his loudest possible voice and reads the roll call of the entire school, from top to bottom. Yes, indeed— it's a Namers on Hills; and once you've responded with "Sum!" as requested, you are free to traipse all the way back to the college and eat your cornflakes.

I like to picture the Trotter siblings and their friend

Alice in the public bar of the St. James Tavern up near Winchester Station, mulling this over:

". . . and then, blow me down, once they've all got up to the top of the blessèd hill, what do they do but turn around and go back down again!" says Pluto Trotter, setting down his pint of mild. "I mean, it's a free country and all, but why do they bother? They could all do with the extra half hour in bed, if you ask me. Sleep like stones, that lot do."

"Well," says Alice, looking at her almost empty glass of rum and black currant, "it takes all sorts, is what I say. Who's for another quick one?"

Belle Trotter looks at her brother, perplexed:

"But Pluto, didn't you say they all read out their names from a book, or somethink? I'm sure you told me they was all doing somethink out loud."

"Well, they might do that, of course," Pluto concedes, "but they could just as easily do it down in the college, like, and save themselves the bother—couldn't they? I mean, they've got all them . . . them quadrangles. Yes, thanks, Alice, I'll have a pint of mild if you're buying."

"Pluto!" His sister is his watchdog. "How many have you had already?"

"Oh go on, Belle—let him have his fun. It's Saturday night—the young gentlemen'll have to wake themselves up tomorrow—it's Sunday, innit?"

"Well, all right I suppose—give him a shandy, Alice, I can't see any harm in that."

"Blimey, Belle—you're on duty tonight, aintcha? Get us a mild, Alice love. The lemonade takes me funny, it does."

"Pluto Trotter, you're a terror, you are. Ooh look, there's a couple of egg and cress left: anybody fancy one?"

In a discreet corner of the saloon bar, meanwhile, the petite old lady with the blue hat and pink lipstick could not possibly be Nora Duplock; nor could her companion in the bow tie, trilby hat, and horn-rimmed spectacles be Mr. Hodges . . . not by any stretch of the imagination.

Under the Floorboards with Fletcher

———

The autumn term begins in summer and ends in winter. Melancholy gathers as the evenings draw in and mists rise in the water meadows. By degrees the air chills and the sunsets move east, toward the Hill. This year, the government experiments with not putting the clocks back in late October, so the waning of daylight hours is a little more gentle than usual. The sunsets of 1967 are particularly vivid: flaming pink, orange, and purple silhouette the trees rising out of the white miasma. This particular autumn feels more wistful than usual—perhaps because the momentum of the previous few years has just peaked, here in 1967. Right on cue, the Kinks release their most intricate song to date, "Autumn Almanac." Much will be written about this era in the future (and here I am adding to the pile), but even as it happens there's a feeling of "Where do we go from here?" in the air.

One place to go, at Winchester College, is into the early morning, ahead of the traffic of the day. Occasionally some inmates rise early, while it's still dark (before Mr. Trotter sallies forth), to finish essays that are due or to revise for an upcoming test. Or simply to have a little time to themselves, while there's nobody much about. Our nocturnal community is small and sustained by instant coffee. With a little ingenuity it's also possible to escape your house altogether and rendezvous with the groovers of other hives—or even the Outside World.

Between the groovers and the meatheads lie the semi-groovers. Semi-groovers are literate boys with good taste who nonetheless have some conventional tendencies: they're not planning to grow their hair down to their navels or smoke themselves into a hashish coma when they leave—and they may even wear ties in their free time. They pick what they like from the available (or elusive) rafts of grooverdom and pad, independent, through their teens, thinking for themselves. Now that's another sentence that's pure Winchester, innit?

One such fellow is Hobson, with whom I find myself sitting halfway up the Hill one sunny autumn afternoon. Hobson is a gentle bear of a fellow with unambitious hair who continues to wear his pale-green sports jacket outside school hours. It's as if he'd been born at the age of forty-seven. He wears thick spectacles and speaks with a subtle emphasis on certain words, as if they're a joke to which only you and he are party:

"Well, Robyn, have you *heard* the *Velvet Underground?* They're really good. Really *good . . .*"

We both stare across the Itchen Valley, at the great gray cross of Winchester Cathedral and the smoke twisting up from chimneys. I grunt that I have yet to hear the Velvet Underground but would certainly like to.

"I know someone from America who's *got* a copy: we could sit under the floorboards and listen one morning. Do you know *Fletcher?*"

I don't really know Fletcher, but I've seen him around the place. He's a tall, intense person with a shock of curly hair growing upward on his head like a flame.

"Fletcher's a *good* guy once you get to know him. His aunt has given him a *whiskey cake* and we're planning to eat it under the floorboards at four o'clock next Sunday morning. Would you like to come *along?*"

I run into Fletcher in one of the cloisters that we all pass through day and night. He has strong cheekbones and his hair is more vertical than ever:

"Oh . . . Hitchcock, isn't it? Yes, Hobson SAID that YOU might be—urHAK!—JOINING us."

I say that I might indeed if that's okay with them:

"Well it's okay with ME and I ASSUME it's okay with Mr. Hobson or he wouldn't have—urHAK!—ASKED."

Fletcher, too, has a way of emphasizing certain words that's punctuated by unpredictable guffaws:

"Of course, whether it's going to be okay with Blotto, Gazebo, and the CHIMP is something I hope we never find OUT—urHAK!"

Blotto being my housemaster, Gazebo being Hobson's, and the Chimp, of course, being Fletcher's. None of them would be at all pleased to discover that we were on the loose in the middle of the night, breaking and entering into each other's prisons. Nonetheless, the absence of Mr. Trotter on Sunday mornings means that the keys to the metal bars by our outside toilets in G House are lying in a vase in the smoky cave that is Blotto's study; all you have to do is sneak in there, take the keys, and unlock the padlock yourself. Nobody seems to notice, certainly not Blotto, who is exhaling his tobacco, pasta, and red-wine fumes peacefully next to his wry Finnish wife at that early hour. Usually.

So next Sunday morning at 4 a.m. I sneak the keys, slide back the metal grid, and step into the exercise yard. G House looms above me, totally black against the somber sky. No light shines from Miss Duplock's quarters, nor from the forty-odd sleeping teenagers who I've just escaped; and Gazebo's house, right over the wall, is just as dark: like a giant prison ship berthed next to ours. Lacking the gymnastic skills to scramble over the wall, despite the best efforts of Mr. Hodges ("Now, your Uncle Hodges would be the first to help you break out of any stalag, you know that, Flight Officer Hitchcock"), I walk through the bike shed and out onto the road.

What a feeling! The wind sighs through the creaking trees and the leaves spiral into the night sky, fluttering like bats. Everything is outlines, there's no depth of vision. The air feels clean, and the streetlights are off. I walk around the block, past the curves of the dingy music school, and turn left down the Gazebo house garden path. As this building begins to tower over me, a low window opens and a voice hisses out my name: "Psst, Robyn—in here, quick!"

In I clamber through a window that I could never find again in daylight, past the parallel clutter of Gazebo's house—similar to our own in G House, but laid out differently—and Hobson, wielding a flashlight, abruptly stops in a corner of their hall. He turns with his finger to his lips, his eyes glinting behind his specs like two cartoon goldfish:

"It's down *there*," he whispers. "Fletcher's already in place." He points to the floorboards, then stoops to fumble with them. A neat square of flooring lifts up—there's a trapdoor in the middle of Gazebo's hall: Wow! How cool is that? I wish we had one in G House. Come to think of it, maybe we do; could that be a way to Mr. Trotter's lair?

My speculations are dissolved by the sound of church organ music wafting up from below, and a faint glow of candlelight.

"After you," whispers Hobson. My feet take me down a very short series of steps into a subterranean chamber. You can't stand up in here. Hunched in a corner next to yet another portable gramophone (cassette players haven't reached Hampshire yet) sits Fletcher, his fountain of hair silhouetted by a candle. An LP is spinning in the shadows beside him, the grooves just catching a flicker of the candlelight as they turn. Hobson lowers the trapdoor and the three of us are soon sitting cross-legged, in a ceremonial fashion.

"What's this record?" I mumble. Lately I've been adopting the passive, dreamy tones used by the Scholars and high-level groovers. This is largely a reaction to the braying, entitled upper-class tones that are part of the deal with boarding schools: the groovers, being essentially hippies, want to distance themselves from these posh donkeys. I figure that, as a semi-groover already, I have a shot at achieving True Grooverdom. This isn't a conscious effort—it's just that, Winchester being a hierarchical place, you always seem to find yourself on some kind of ladder.

But Fletcher sees through this straightaway:

"Oh GOD, Hitchcock, you sound like one of those FUCKING Scholars! Ur-HAK! It's Olivier Messiaen, he's a COMPOSER, for God's sake."

"Uh, actually, Fletch," interjects Hobson gently, "we should probably keep it down—ceilings have *ears*, you know?" And he points above his head to the time-soaked boards that run above us. Fletcher's volume immediately halves:

"Oh, great God in a gondola—you're absolutely RIGHT, of course. Scratch that, folks: let's take it down to a subsonic MUMBLE." Fletcher leans forward across the sandy detritus that makes up the floor in this grotto, and hisses the next sentence with conspiratorial venom: "I mean, if the CHIMP was running this house he'd be directly above us with a PERISCOPE—ur-HAK!"

We are three little old teenagers: each of us is experimenting with his voice, searching for who to become. At least, maybe Hobson and I are; Fletcher is simply Fletcher, and will never be anything else.

Messiaen's organ music plays on, quietly, and for a while I sit and mime to enjoying it. Like my father, I love a good tune and lyrics to draw me in. Symphonies, fugues, sonatas, and the like are hard for me to grasp— too intricate for my peasant ears, or my reptile brain. But this record sounds exactly right in a subterranean grotto.

"Mmmf!" exclaims Fletcher as one side of the record ends: "I suppose I should open Aunt Jane's CAKE. Would either of you care for a SLICE?"

The Velvet Underground turns out not to be on the menu this Sunday morning, but as Fletcher distributes

Aunt Jane's cake, Hobson slides another record onto the portable shrine and clicks it into action.

"You might *like* this one, Robyn," he confides, his lenses twinkling in the candlelight. "It's the signs of the zodiac—*Cosmic Sounds*. They're all quite *fun* except for Pisces, the last one. What's your *sign*, do you think?"

It turns out that I *am* a Pisces, according to the record cover, which I can just decipher in the dim orange light. I've never thought about astrology before. Then the music begins: sitars and synthesizers provide a state-of-the-art 1967 backing for a theatrical American male voice:

"Nine times, the color red / Explodes like heated blood / The battle is on! . . . Aries is first to face the flames."

This is more like it. As the spicy, esoteric whiskey cake finds our throats, the Hollywood mysticism finds our ears, and the candlelight just about finds our eyes. The synesthesia is complete, and even without the presence of Eno or any fully qualified groover, this is definitely a Happening.

"Oh GOD, what IS this music? Hobson, where do you FIND this stuff?" Fletcher whispers a muffled cackle through a mouthful of cake.

"A circle is perfect / But the world isn't round / Virgo can prove it," intones the American voice, serenely. I close my eyes and straighten my back, as if I was meditating.

"Glad you approve," murmurs Hobson, holding his

slice of cake away from his face like a pipe: "When is *your* birthday, James?"

James? Ye gods! Fletcher has a first name? He seems so indelibly Fletcher.

"Why, it's tomorrow, actually," says Fletcher thoughtfully. "That's why Aunt Jane sent me this CAKE, come to think of it."

Hobson is perusing the LP sleeve: "Hmmm, that makes you . . . let's have a look." He takes off his glasses and squints right up close to the album sleeve: "Yes, that makes you a Scorpio."

"To be afraid / And not care that you are afraid / Is the courage of which Scorpio is made," declaims the American voice, right on cue.

"Oh GOD, roll me in BEESWAX, but I actually think I'd prefer to be listening to Country Joe and the FISH, ker-HAK."

Interlude in Camden Passage

———

It's November and the year is dying. The purple tissue paper I've pinned over the windows in my parents' new attic to enhance the dayglo sunsets is faded already. I have lovingly cut out the Peter Blake postcard and face mask from the cardboard insert in my copy of *Sgt. Pepper* and pinned them to a wooden beam up there. One afternoon I tear them up in a fit.

Occasionally, I still destroy my favorite things—just a few of them, not all I possess, and I still don't know why. The Bob Dylan poster in my bedroom will go the same way in a few months. Feelings are hard to contain, and my family don't know how to express them either. So . . . where can they go? On a good day into music, in my case.

At school I'm now taking weekly guitar lessons from a genial old fellow with a wispy mustache; he's called Mr. Dacre. He has three bent-back fingers on his right hand, from what must have been a painful accident; so his classical guitar technique is limited. I am slow to read music, and his memory is patchy, so he basically gives me the same lesson every week. Mr. Dacre does, however, teach me how to tune my guitar, or, at least, what the notes should be if I can get them in tune. Now I can play along to my LPs with greater confidence even though I don't know any chords yet.

"Can you actually play that thing, Hitchcock?" inquires Mudfellow, poking his head around the door as I sit practicing in an empty dormitory. "Or is it playing you?"

Just you wait, Mudfellow. One day. Nothing is conscious in my head, in terms of planning. My instinct is to play the guitar, long before I've *learned* how to play it. Why bother with mastering the act of walking if your goal is to run? How else can you learn, but by playing? I'm magnetized by the guitar; it's become my compass.

The year is dying, though it doesn't seem like the same one that started life eleven months ago. Is it really only six months since I first heard Jimi Hendrix in the abandoned pigsties? Was that even me, listening to that little transistor, in my purple nylon shirt? The early colors of the year seem so muted now, looking back. How weird existence must have been without a portable record player. It feels like life has crashed an invisible barrier somewhere. I've become the me that I'll be for the rest of my life; the kid in the purple shirt was a caterpillar from which I've hatched. Or a pupa, perhaps.

As the leaves fall and the nights draw in, the first Pink Floyd LP is in heavy rotation on the House Gramophone:

the somber mania of Syd Barrett and his cohorts burrows into the varnished surfaces and resounds all winter. While the instrumental track "Pow R. Toc H." plays in the other room, a senior groover (he's about to turn seventeen) gives his take from his little study off the wooden corridor down which I first clattered the previous January:

"Yeah, man, this Pink Floyd shit is just pop music on one level, you know? But listen to that piano—that's jazz! It's all starting to merge . . . it's too much, maaan, heh-heh," and like all true groovers he mocks his very grooverdom with a little giggle at the end.

Most groovers are big into Second Childhood: this is confusing for me as I'm barely out of my first childhood.

"Ah, too much, man—it's an ice cream!"

"Oh, wow, look—it's a sausage!"

"Far out, Robyn: have you been watching *The Magic Roundabout*?"

I am beginning to fixate on LP covers. So much of what is sacred in life is housed inside them, and right now they're particularly vivid. On a visit up to London for the second micro-interval that term, I've been invited to stay in Islington with some fellow art-bourgeois friends of my parents; they live just off Camden Passage, which is a quaint, eighteenth-century cobbled side street, too narrow for motor vehicles. This makes it perfect for antique market stalls and boutiques.

One of these is Hang-Up, London's first ever poster shop, which has opened this very autumn. Within half an hour I'm there, in fluorescent heaven.

Hang-Up is the closest I've yet been to being *inside* an album cover—discounting the ivy nooks that I occasionally lurk in when I'm pretending to be one of the Incredible String Band. The shop is suffused with incense, and posters cover the walls. My eyes are drawn to a golden one, on which Jimi Hendrix is depicted as a Native American with a feather headdress and a long peace pipe. His rhythm section, Mitch and Noel, are on the distant skyline in a shower of UFOs. The three musicians are printed in dark blue against a pink and orange dayglo sunset—it's breathtaking. All the horizons of 1967 are in that poster, and it costs less than an LP to buy.

Various people are milling around in the shop, in a kind of slow motion. I don't know if they work there, are customers, or if they themselves are for sale. Everybody seems to be some kind of exhibit. They rustle and murmur—nobody talks at full volume. It's as if we're mannequins on a riverbed, rippling upward like waterweed.

"Are you a fan of Jimi's?" asks the man behind the counter as he wraps the poster for me in a cardboard tube.

"Oh yes! I mean—yeah, I think so, man," I respond, hauling out my best mumble.

"Oh well, see that guy over there? He designed Jimi's new album cover. Go and say hello—he won't bite."

I sidle over to a mannequin who has exploding hair. From below the neck, he's swathed in an old military coat. He peers at me through circular glasses, though they aren't blue. He doesn't bite, and is more than happy to explain how he fashioned the cover for *Axis: Bold As Love*. I'm really flattered that he thinks I'm worth talking to, as I'm obviously only a groover in training. However, the more he tries to explain how he seamlessly merged Jimi's face with an old Indian image of elephant gods, the more lost I become. Basically, the cover artist is describing airbrushing, a technique that Stalin used to smoothly erase ex-colleagues from Russian Politburo photographs. *(Nowadays it's called Photoshop; in years to come it may be called Mother.)*

I walk back toward my hosts' place with the Hendrix

poster scrolled in my left fist. The autumn afternoon is gliding toward another flaming sunset. Camden Passage is thronged with metro-groovers; everything here in London is more vivid than in the damp flint citadels of Winchester. It's Saturday, and the market is in bloom. Victoriana is now valuable: what has been junk for sixty years is now a cool prize.

The old and middle-aged men and women whose young lives were hijacked by fighting their near neighbor, Germany, twice in thirty years, are naturally upset to see us hairy, effete noncombatants donning the epaulettes and stripes *Sgt. Pepper*–style: yeah, we all look a little like military men. Are we mocking them, and all they did for us? Not intentionally, no, but what do we care? They were in the wars, we aren't. Time has moved on. And in the market stalls in Camden Passage I discover hundreds of tiny wristwatch faces—watches from a hundred dead wrists—prized loose from their circular mountings and straps, on sale for 6d each. And they still work—the clockwork still ticks! This to me is an immense bargain. The clockfaces themselves are the size of a shilling, and half the price: yaysville! I buy six of them for three bob and take them back to glue to pieces of balsa wood in my cubicle at the college. They will look great with the faux-stained-glass lampshade I'm building there using sweet wrappers. Unless I smash them up . . .

Back at the Islington house, a gradual party is underway. In the front room, the daylight fades onto a couple of people who are in there with me. A middle-aged bloke introduces me to a younger woman:

"This is Cathy—she produces a TV series called *A Whole Scene Going*."

"Oh wow—really?"

More descriptions ensue, that I can't easily follow. They're drinking red wine; I haven't quite got to that stage yet. The Forest of Dean in me smells pretension, but the groover in me is panting like a sheepdog at the leash. This, goddammit, is a scene! Through the membrane of my own reactions, I'm also aware that this metropolitan life would have been mine if my parents hadn't defected to the home counties when I was six months old. But my parents are essentially shy folk, and being shy is probably as much as they both can agree on.

The conversation makes its way to a casual bombshell:

"I mean, for instance: Ringo smokes a lot of pot."

The man takes a swig of his wine and looks around for a refill.

"Really? Ringo Starr smokes pot?"

"Oh yeah, he's a big pot smoker. Huge. He's stoned all the time."

I am staggered. Maybe Ringo, too, knows the meaning of life?

It's Getting Very Near the End

———

B ack at the college, and around the world, the Beatles are keeping us company. The leaves are all but fallen, and the *Magical Mystery Tour* EP has replaced *Sgt. Pepper* on the House Gramophone. Snow falls on the ancient walls, purple in the glow of dusk, and the whole place looks like it did when I first arrived early last year. But now it's become my place: I'm embedded here, in its hierarchy and the reflexes that it's carved into me. I am now 50 percent Winchester College and 50 percent Bob Dylan. But where is he?

Nora Duplock wouldn't know. A bunch of us catch the flu and are in her sickroom.

"If you could only keep still, I could put the thermometer into your mouth. Dearie me—keep still, can't you!"

"Sorry, Miss Duplock."

"Oh, heavens—there's four of you in here and I've no hands but my own. There . . ." She extracts the icicle-thin tube from my warm gums. "Well, it's still over one hundred—you'd best stay here again for tonight. What's that awful music?"

Harpo has a radio, which for some reason is allowed in the sickroom, though not in the main house. A Pink Floyd song comes on that I haven't heard before: "Free games for May / See-ee-ee-ee Emily play." It floats across the dead room like the breath of life, then it's gone. I haven't heard it on the House Gramophone. Then comes a song called "The Letter" by the Box Tops, which is pretty great, too—urgent and makes you want to get out of bed. The singer is a very young guy called Alex Chilton, not much older than we are.

From our sickbeds Harpo and I are discussing Dylan's song "Visions of Johanna," which has become my prayer.

"It's on electric guitar, I reckon," I assert.

"No, you think so? That's totally an acoustic, Robyn."

"Well, okay, it's acoustic to begin with . . ."

"So it's basically acoustic, then, isn't it?"

In later years, Harpo will become a lawyer.

And I will become a songwriter. "Like a Rolling Stone" hooks me, "Desolation Row" pulls me in, and "Visions of Johanna" . . . more subtle, more engulfing: it *becomes* me. I want to melt the barrier between myself and that song, though I don't know yet where that will take me. The snaffling bass in the version on *Blonde on Blonde*, the snapping drums, and the cracking guitar that punctuates it (to this day nobody can confirm who plays that: Robbie Robertson? Jerry Kennedy? Wayne Moss? Charlie

McCoy? Nobody that I ask in Nashville seems to know for sure), Al Kooper's spooky Hammond organ—and the words! The mood goes up as it goes down. I spin around and make myself dizzy listening to them: in the same verse infinity goes up on trial, and the jellyfish women all sneeze. Although it turns out on closer examination that they're jelly-faced; regardless, they can't find their knees. And, to be on the safe side, name me someone who's not a parasite, and I'll go out and say a prayer for them. With that kind of insight, Bob Dylan was—I mean, where the hell is he?

"He's been in a car crash," two Maltese girls told me in the sea the year before. That was all I heard of him for a year, then a headline, DELVING DEEP INTO THE DYLAN MYSTERY, caught my eye in the *Record Mirror*. Like all habits, reading the music press has snuck up on me and now it's planted in my hypothalamus. Finally I'm rewarded, a month before Christmas, by a piece in *Melody Maker*, the hippest of our weekly music papers: EXCLUSIVE! NICK JONES LISTENS TO SEVEN SECRET TAPES. I can't believe it: without any warning, Dylan has casually sent over to Britain some new songs that—my mind broils with joy and disbelief—he has no plan to release. WTF! I memorize the article, cut it out from the paper, and sleep with it below my pillow.

"What's that wank pad you've got under there, Hitchcock?"

"Nothing you'd want, Mudfellow."

Most intriguing is a reference to Nashville: Dylan himself—alive as you or me—has been seen at a Ramada Inn (what's a Ramada Inn?) wearing a hat (is he going bald?) and with an ear-to-ear beard (how long would it take me to grow one: two years?). He has been recording at Columbia Studios, Nashville, Tennessee. So he's still here, in this world, roughly three thousand miles west of Winchester: stars of joy! And the word is that he's sounding less cynical, less harsh, but still unfathomable—as deep as ever. And if he's written some new songs, they are pretty much certain to reveal the meaning of life: if he doesn't reveal it, who will? If only I could get to Nashville; maybe Dylan has already revealed it to somebody who works at the Ramada Inn?

I picture him there, enigmatically sipping a pint of lager and lime, with all the knowledge of the world in his eyes. In my reverie, I picture myself there too, standing silently at his side, looking up at him like a faithful hound. Although as Dylan is nearly a foot shorter than I am by now, I'd have to look faithfully downward.

"What's up, man?" says Bob, registering that I'm there. In reality, I would be sweating with nerves and too in awe to speak. But you can be your best self in a dream.

"Well, Mr. Dylan," I respond calmly, "I'm from Winchester in England—"

"'Winchester Cathedral'—you know that song?" Dylan interrupts, smiling at me: "'Winchester Cathedral, you're bringing me down—you stood and you watched as my baby left town.' I dig that song! Do you dig that song?"

"Er, well, yes . . . I, uh . . . my dad has a copy, actually."

"Boy, I bet he does." Dylan grins beneath his hat. The beard is quite sparse and gingery: "Being watched by a cathedral—that must be something, y'know?"

"Well, I was reading in the *Melody Maker* that—"

"The *Melody Maker*?" Dylan cracks up. "Hey, that's Max Jones—he writes for that paper—is he a friend of yours? Or is he a friend of your dad's?"

"Er, well . . . no, but I mean . . ." My reverie is more confusing than I'd anticipated. "The article I read was by Nick Jones, not Max."

Dylan freezes in midswig of his lager and lime. He fixes me with his hypnotic Medusa snake eyes:

"I don't know any Nick Jones. What does he want, this Nick Jones?"

"Well, he wrote that you'd recorded some new songs."

"Well, so what if I have, man? I'm a songwriter, that's what songwriters do best, y'know—we write songs, and we record them, if they're *good* enough."

Struggling to master my own fantasy, I force myself to get to the point: "Well, Nick Jones says—ah, forget it—look, Mr. Dylan, in total confidence and between ourselves: could you tell me the meaning of life?"

Dylan's face changes again, and relaxes somewhat. He puts down his lager and looks at his wristwatch:

"Y'know, man, it's amazing this thing works at all. People steal the clockfaces from them all the time. Listen," he says gently, "I have to go now. I may be some time. Just remember, kid, that it's all up here." He taps his own forehead and then lightly taps mine. "Just keep it safe and dry in there and nobody can take it from you. Nobody. Take care, man, and say hello to Max Jones from me."

He puts down his glass, not quite drained, spins on his heel, and vanishes through the revolving doors of the Ramada Inn. I contemplate finishing his pale golden drink, then I, too, vanish from my daydream.

In the Art Room, the Ugly Pullover shuffles up to me:

"Hey, Robyn, could you make us a poster for our gig?"

"Your gig, Pullover?"

"Yeah, man, it's next Monday, in the College Cellars. We're all gonna be there. It'll be a trip, heh-heh."

This is very exciting: I'm being incorporated into a Happening—little me, who is half from the Forest of Dean! "Yes, man, of course. What's your band called?" Nineteen sixty-seven is the year that groups become bands, and moreover dispense with having "The" as a prefix.

"Ah, man, our band is usually called the Earth, y'know?" he mumbles exquisitely, and I lower my own voice to echo him:

"The Earth? Right, that's cool."

"Yeah, but this will be a special event: it's featuring a guy called Adrian Gruber," says the Pullover, with an air of mystery. "He's from Otherwhere, heh-heh."

"Wow. Where's that?"

"Wherever you want it to be, man: just use your imagination—you have plenty of it."

A week later, it's the last morning of the long winter term, around 6 a.m. I've clambered out of Blotto's house, stomped past the ghostly sewage works, and am now on top of St. Catherine's Hill. The lights of Winchester flicker up through the damp darkness. A dirty orange glow on the horizon marks the nearby city of Southampton. Around a bonfire right at the center of the ring of trees sit about seven groovers. But where is Fletcher? He assured me he was coming, with a consignment of rare French cheeses from his great-uncle Bartholomew:

"If you enjoyed the CAKE, Hitch, you will positively COMBUST when you sample Uncle Bart's BRIE. Good God, man, it's so RUNNY you can practically DRINK it, ur-HAK!"

But I've been here for ages and there's no sign of him. I set my alarm for 4 a.m. and assume that he did the same.

"Don't fret, man," says Jansch. "He's probably just been picked up by a UFO."

"And it's bound to drop him off again—they're very reliable," says Simon, twinkling in the firelight. "More reliable than buses."

"Are they?" I ask, quite seriously. "That's just as well: you'd never get a bus to come up this hill."

"Oh, yeah, man—totally," says the Ugly Pullover, pacing the encampment like a night watchman in his long military coat. "This is a Neolithic site. Somewhere up here are buried Druids . . ."

"Yeah, probably hundreds of them," adds Simon.

"Hundreds of Druids," adds Galen. "All encased in lint."

"Linty Druids—wow, man."

"Er, how do you know they were wrapped in lint?"

"Ah, look, Robyn, you don't want to get hung up on the details. The point is that Neolithic sites like this have always attracted UFOs."

"Really?" I want to believe everything I'm told. And perhaps the Druids had magnetic skeletons . . .

"Oh yeah, man. Did you know that Pink Floyd attracts UFOs?"

I can believe that, totally.

"Spacecraft have been coming here for centuries," says Jansch, throwing a bunch of twigs on the fire. A shower of sparks and heat swirls up in the cold night air. "So your friend will be fine. I expect they'll drop him off at a weird hour, though: time is different for them."

If Fletcher is in a UFO, what will the aliens make of his cheese? I wonder.

Talk turns to Adrian Gruber. As requested, I drew a pen-and-ink poster for the event, which went up on the noticeboard at Flint Court. The gig took place but I wasn't allowed to attend as it was in the College Cellars after dark, and I'm technically too young to wander the looming masonry at night. This is a real bummer—I was dying to go. Senior groovers from most of the houses went; although a few houses like Dopey's and the Shoveler's are so uncool that they contain no groovers at all. Tragically.

"So what did Adrian Gruber play, in the end?" I ask. "Or was he just singing?"

"Well," says Simon, "he played all the instruments, and he sang—and so did we."

"I don't get it—how could he play everything at once?"

"Ah look, man," says the Ugly Pullover, "you don't need to be so literal about everything, you know? Heh-heh."

"Yeah," adds Simon, "Adrian Gruber isn't bounded by specifics . . ."

". . . he's in everything . . ."

". . . omnipresent . . ."

". . . in everyone and everything at once, you dig?"

I frown into the fallen leaves composting around us in the dark. The birds are beginning to sing.

"Do you mean: he doesn't really exist? There's no such person?"

"On the contrary, man—he does more than exist: he's in all of us. We're all Adrian Gruber."

"What, even Hodges?" This gets a laugh.

"Oh, especially Hodges, yes."

"He's totally Gruber."

So Adrian Gruber is an imaginary creature, like Sherlock Holmes. He can never die as he was never born, except from Simon's head, like the goddess Athena. Adrian Gruber is an idea; what would Granny have made of that?

The Scholars hold every idea up to the light and squint at it, assessing it in a detached way. Life is a movie seen from a great distance—entertaining or disturbing, it never totally engulfs them. This seems to me like perfection. I slither back down the Hill as dawn seeps through the wet sky. No sunlight intrudes.

A few days later, I'm back at my parents' house, enjoying the central heating, when the telephone rings.

"Robyn, darling—yoo-hoo! There's a James on the phone for you . . ."

A James? I don't know any James. But I don't get many phone calls, so I shuffle down to the shiny gray dial phone mounted on the library wall:

"Hitch?"

Ye gods—it's Fletcher: has the UFO dropped him off at home? I wonder.

"Heya, Fletch—what happened? The college guys said you'd been abducted by a UFO."

"Oh GOD! I was abducted all right, but it was by BLOTTO."

"Blotto? Does he have a spaceship?"

"I wish he DID! No, I was just crawling through your bloody changing-room window at about half past THREE in the morning when Blotto appeared, pretty fucking HAMMERED by the looks of him, and we were face-to-face, er-HAK."

"Oh, jeez—and you were looking for me? But I thought we were meeting on the Hill."

"Well, technically we were, but I was early so I thought I'd drop in."

"Oh Christ—you dropped in to Blotto . . . he was still up?"

"I dropped in to Blotto. He was VERY still up. He practically dropped his PIPE: 'What the HELL are you doing?'"

A shiver of self-interested paranoia flashed through me:

"Well . . . I mean . . . you were here to see me, weren't you?"

"Oh, he was beyond THAT. I blew whatever remained of his SATURATED mind: he just frog-marched me out his front door and gave me the heave-ho."

"Phew—thank God for that. So why didn't you come up to the Hill?"

Fletcher inhaled and blew a straw of deep venom through his nostrils:

"Because, Hitch—before he passed out, he telephoned to the CHIMP who was waiting for me with a HORSE-WHIP when I got back to the house. Waiting, moreover, in his deathly pajamas and FLYING HELMET, and grunted at me that—oh, hang on—mmmmpf, mmmmpf," the unmistakable sound of Fletcher ingesting an emergency mouthful of Brie came down the wire, "if I wanted to escape being EXPELLED I had to read the ENTIRE fucking WORKS of Jane Austen during the holidays. He's awaiting me with a special Fletcher exam customized for just that purpose on my return."

"Sheesh, Fletch—that's heavy."

"Heavy indeed, Hitch: I've just ingested *Sense and Sensibility* and it gives me the deep HEAVES—er-HAK."

The English novelist Jane Austen lived and died in Winchester, just as the Industrial Revolution gathered momentum and Britain became a nation of coal and steel. In years to come, Miss Austen's stories will be adapted for Hollywood movies. Fletcher is not a fan.

At my parents' house on December 26, 1967, Christmas is taking its toll and my father is feeling overtly suicidal and discreetly homicidal this Boxing Day evening. He is suffering from too much of his mother—two whole days' worth—while my mother is missing hers, in a silent way. The family takes refuge in the television, as families do.

"So what are we watching now, Robyn lovie?"

I'm sitting in front of the black-and-white television wearing the orange kaftan that my mother has lovingly gifted me for Christmas.

"It's the Beatles, Mum."

The *Magical Mystery Tour* film is being shown for the first time ever. My legs are crossed in a kind of lotus position. My sisters are next to me on the floor, concentrating on the box in front of us.

"Ooh my," says Grandma, "the Beatles again. I think I might go and look at how the mince pies are doing."

My father is already on his feet, lurching around to pick up the last of the discarded Christmas wrapping paper. It's not easy gathering up rubbish if one of your legs won't bend, but anything's better than being stuck in front of the TV full of yet another meal you didn't need, surrounded by your mother *and* your family.

Yet somehow the Beatles manage to draw them all in, to prevent their escape. "Your Mother Should Know" strikes a chord with my mum, who is missing her mum:

"Oh, I like that one, Robyn lovie, the one that goes, 'Your mother should know'—what's its title, do you think?"

"'Your Mother Should Know,' Mum."

"Mmm, yes . . . ahhh . . . is it?"

"Yes, Mum."

When John Lennon loads up the spaghetti on Auntie Jessie's plate and the pasta sauce gets all over their clothes, Grandma comments:

"Ooh my, Robyn—they'll be needing Daisy Damp-wash after all that."

"Who's Daisy Dampwash, Grandma?"

"Well, I never—haven't you heard of her?"

I grunt a reply, already sinking back into the Beatles.

"Well, Daisy Dampwash was what we called the laundry in our day."

The film soon ends and we disperse, as much as a family can in midwinter. I enjoy *Magical Mystery Tour*—the world and I have been listening to the songs for a month already and we love them all. However, it was filmed in color but at this point everyone in Britain still has a black-and-white TV, unless you're as wealthy as the Beatles, or maybe Peter Sellers. But you don't become rich to be like everybody else, do you?

It's not until the newspaper reviews come out the next day that the nation learns that *Magical Mystery Tour* wasn't good after all. Too bad . . .

. . . but never mind: Bob Dylan's new LP, *John Wesley Harding,* is finally coming out soon, as the bleak new year cracks like a gray egg over Britain. The long-awaited bible on how to live our lives: I am counting on all the fundamental answers to the questions that life poses being etched into that black vinyl disc.

And just like that, 1967 is . . .

It's Getting Very Near the End, Take 2

———

Fifty-six years later, Fletcher and I are sitting in a chilly London back garden at midnight. On my lap is a spaniel, so Fletcher cradles the cheese.

"Well, I actually can't REMEMBER, is the absolute truth, whether I went up the Hill in the end that morning."

Nor does he have any memory of being in a UFO—but who does? They stopped flying after that winter, anyway.

"But I DO remember what I said to Blotto, when he found me in the changing room."

"Oh really?"

Fletcher reaches for the cheddar and cuts himself a thick slice, which he squeezes onto some toast.

"Oh yes . . . mmmpf . . . mmmpf. Blotto said, 'What the hell are you doing here?' and I replied, 'I'd rather not SAY, sir.'"

"Wow—that was plucky. How did Blotto respond?"

"Oh God, Hitch—I'm sorry to say I can't remember THAT, either."

"Oh, well—that 'I'd rather not say' is masterful—I'll definitely put that in the book."

"Be my guest. But one thing I DO know—Blotto didn't telephone to the CHIMP until the next DAY!"

Oh . . . I'm nonplussed to think I've misremembered this sequence of events. How much else have I got wrong about what actually went down in 1967? I wonder.

It's Getting Very Near the End, Take 3

In the breakfast area of the Ramada Inn in Nashville sit three British tourists. It's 9 a.m. and they've been awake for hours. Dawn comes faster in Tennessee than in southern England, and they are hungry with jet lag. Belle Trotter surveys the menu that she's clasping with both sturdy hands, one each side of the laminated cardboard:

"Blimey, Pluto—it's eggs as far as the eye can see here."

"Not much different back home, then, is it?" says her brother, lighting the second cigarette of the morning.

"Pluto Trotter! Put that out—it'll ruin your appetite."

"Ah, leave him be, Belle," murmurs Alice, eyes still fixed on her menu. "He's on holiday now."

"Oh, I dunno, Alice," sighs Pluto as a silver feather of smoke from his new-lit Player's No. 6 curls up toward the ceiling: "Them eggs just follow me around, don't they? I'm always scrambling them for the young gentlemen, ain't I? Only . . . eggs look a bit different over here . . ."

"You're right there," agrees Alice, pointing at her menu

with a finely lacquered cerise fingernail. "Here, what's 'over easy' mean?"

"Let's have a look," murmurs Belle, reaching for Alice's menu.

"Oi! You've got your own menu, love—plenty to go round here . . ."

"Silly me!" responds Belle.

Pluto Trotter scratches the top of his head.

"Well, I never knew an egg you couldn't crack."

"Pluto—you mind yourself with that fag of yours, else you'll burn your scalp," says his sister, ever the protector.

"Yeah, but I mean 'eggs over easy'—that means they're not always easy. How difficult can an egg be, you know what I mean?"

"Oh," says a smoky American voice just above them, "they're just fried eggs upside down, y'know?"

A man in a broad-brimmed hat has materialized by their table, looking over their jet-lagged shoulders. He doesn't seem to be a waiter, with his patchy beard and his eyes like two blue marbles. Nonetheless, for a moment he stares down at the three of them, as if expecting something.

"Ooh—is that nice, them eggs like that?"

"Well," the newcomer's head raises up to peer around the four corners of the ceiling, then lowers to the table again, "I never stray far from them for long, ma'am—that's for sure."

The stranger tips his hat to the three Brits and strides away to the hotel lobby.

"Well, I dunno—I might give 'em a go. I'm dead peckish, I am. What about you girls, then? Seeing as we're here . . ."

Belle looks around for a waitress, and various egg meals are soon ordered. Alice is pensively watching a green and red stuffed parrot perched in a plastic oak tree, beneath a Confederate flag.

"He looks familiar, don't you think?"

"What, that parrot?"

"Nah—the geezer in the hat, the eggs-over-easy bloke."

"Oh yes . . . that fellow: he's a local, must be. Always good to pick up a tip from a local—saves yer time, you know?"

"Ye-es, maybe. You know what?"

"What, Alice?"

"I recognize him. He's a pop singer, he is."

"Go on! He looks like a vicar or summat, I reckon. Don't you think, Belle?"

Belle has her mind on breakfast and is negotiating her way around her second refill of American black coffee.

"I think," says Alice, "it's that pop singer . . . what's his name . . . Donovan."

It's Getting Very Near

———

Jansch, Galen, and Simon are edging down the slippery hill, their midnight eyes consummated by the holy dawn. The air is clear, though the sky is cloudy. For an instant, they feel a presence behind them: a metallic dragonfly that hovers and then flits away.

"Wow, man, they're flying low tonight."

"To be high is to be low, and there's an end on it."

"But where shall we three meet again?"

"Our meeting lies ahead of us, shrouded in cornflakes . . ."

". . . and the hebdomadal chanting of the One that . . ."

". . . is Two!"

Then they lustily sing a popular hit of the day, "If I Only Had Time," as they stagger through Kate's Cunt.

"Wait!" exclaims Simon. "Did that really happen—that thing behind us?"

All three sit down in the damp grass and pass a lit No. 6 between them. They are tired, and sleep begins to steal over them.

"Yeah—that spaceship was right behind us . . ."

". . . and we weren't even playing Pink Floyd."

The UFO is hovering over the Solent, a few miles to the south and a thousand feet above the sullen midwinter sea. Inside, the pilot looks down:

"So, what do we do now?"

"Hurry up and wait, mate."

"What about our guest?"

"Our guest, Chief?"

"Our guest—you know, the guy we picked up?"

"Oh gawd—him? He's got all that . . . lactic matter, Chief, you know, that he had when we picked him up? It's stinking the place out."

"Well, we're *intergalactic*, Squire, so . . ."

"Oh, fuck off, Denzil—this 'stuff' is well niffy . . . Oh, hang on a minute: he's coming round."

On the platinum couch, Fletcher awakes:

"Hmm. Oh, yes—my GOD! Is that the BRIE over there? Sweet Jesus in a FRYING pan! Don't let it get away. I mean . . . oh, I beg your pardon . . . where am I?"

The aliens motion to each other:

"Take him back and drop him off, I would. The Great One isn't going to thank us if we take him all the way back home and we smell like this."

"Yeah—I know what you mean. These outlying worlds are a crapshoot at the best of times . . ."

"Hey ho—another day, another dollar . . ."

Fletcher advances toward the two spindly beings at the control panel, proffering a morsel of slippery cheese on a Carr's water biscuit:

"Oh, great GOD in a gondola, gentlemen—just try a BITE of this. It's exQUISITE!"

Epilogue

Nineteen sixty-seven finished, but it never ended.

Bob Dylan, like a loved one who you meet at a station in a dream, returned a few weeks into 1968 as someone else altogether: *John Wesley Harding* was flat, beige, and not much fun to listen to. Hearing it for the first time, hunched over my portable gramophone in a chilly dormitory, I thought: "It's him all right—but he's farther away, and the songs are so short—what's going on?" The exhilaration was gone, he was older and wiser.

Dylan's comeback LP had a wide sonic range, from the bat-squeak of the harmonica to the rumbling of the bass guitar. The lyrics and his masterful sleeve notes hinted that the meaning of life was in there somewhere. Which seemed to be (for male listeners): grow a beard, marry your true love, be a good neighbor, and the world will be all right. In a way, we disciples got our money's worth. Nobody dared say they didn't like it, but *JWH* didn't spend half the time on the record player that *Highway 61* or *Blonde on Blonde* did, and still do.

John Wesley Harding to me signaled the Great Retreat: the Beatles, the Rolling Stones, even acts such as the Doors jettisoned psychedelia and made their way back to rock 'n' roll. Dylan's influence was so immense that wherever he appeared to point, others followed. You could see it unfolding across 1968—and although the rock community took ever more drugs, their music became less experimental. But my school friends and I were now part of a vast market that the record companies, the musicians, and the lifestyle sellers could exploit—and we loved it.

Still, gatefold album sleeves and natty graphics masked increasingly mediocre music, it seemed to me. When I finally started going to gigs later that year—my parents were on the whole tolerant people—I realized that long hair and long guitar solos were no substitute for inspiration. My friends and I also twigged that drugs tended to produce aimless musical sludge; not that this stopped us from smoking hash, or from growing our hair down to our nipples, once we were free of the college hair police.

I finally managed to lose my psychic virginity—I got stoned, which was an overwhelming joy for a while—and then my hetero physical one; I began to get what I had long desired. I was on the path to being one of the big boys. I'd been dying to leave the college; yet the day I finally did leave, in mid-1970, I came home, rolled a cigarette, drank a beer, and lay on my narrow bed at my parents' house, feeling aimless and lost. Winchester College equips you for Winchester College, not for the world outside. I'd been inside just a little too long.

Martz and I had begun to play guitars together in our last years at the college; he has a feel for the way music flows from chord to chord, finding the melody within. After the gates of school had closed behind us, we took refuge from the increasingly weird, exiled life that we found ourselves in by playing music together. At twenty we were like two little old men, composing quaint old-fashioned songs that actually worked best on wealthy middle-aged drunk ladies. Had we been more clued in and responsive we might have made reasonable gigolos. But we did all right busking Beatles songs in London, enough to buy us pizza on a good day.

We went our separate musical ways mid-decade; he sensibly decided not to waste his education and became a lawyer. Martz and I are still friends; better friends than ever, in fact.

Then I drifted up to Cambridge, shorn of all social skills, and began an offensive on the town and college folk clubs. Eventually Morris Windsor, Kimberley Rew, and Matthew Seligman—the key figures of what became the Soft Boys—came into my orbit, and somehow we began to make records. These didn't sell much at the time but they did put us on the map.

All along, I remained rooted in 1967: country rock, glam, funk, disco, reggae, and punk more or less passed me by. As the songwriter and navigator of the Soft Boys, I was happy that we were touted as psychedelic revivalists, even though we weren't really. The soul of the times had changed so much in ten years—we were no more about "love & peace" than the Sex Pistols were; we just used the old musical forms to encase my own take on human hell.

Ten years after leaving Winchester College, I finally made it to New York with the band, and now I really did feel like one of the big boys. Iggy Pop and Mick Ronson were staying at the same hotel as us, although our budget was so tight that all six of our party slept in one room.

The Soft Boys foundered in 1981 but we stayed in touch and the survivors—Kimberley, Morris, and I—still play together in various combinations more than forty years on. Slowly, slowly, ever so slowly as the 1980s unfurled, I began to realize that I was truly living my teenage dream: touring America, releasing records on major labels, getting my nose in the rock 'n' roll trough—this was what I'd read about in *Melody Maker* and *Rolling Stone*. I even did occasional interviews with them. I too recorded albums in Nashville, and eventually made one in London with the great Joe Boyd himself.

All the while, within me I've carried the soul of 1967.

Music budded and came to fruition then in a way that—to my ears—has never been surpassed. Perhaps that's simply because my particular class of "boomers" came of age as the psychedelic upheaval broke through the tarmac of reality. Kids reaching adolescence in the age of Harry Styles surely feel as intensely as we did—but I wonder if they feel as intense about the music made now as we did about its hippie ancestors.

Regardless, I'm grateful that the stopped clock of 1967 ticks on in me—it's given me a job for life.

Acknowledgments

This book was written and edited on my phone entirely between the hours of 1 and 6 a.m., during bouts of sleeplessness. My cats Ringo and Tubby kept me company for the initial draft, so they are the first creatures I have to thank for it. Some of the characters in the narrative are more real than others; I'd particularly like to thank Martin Stanway-Mayers, James Fletcher, Peter "Harpo" Harrop, and Galen Strawson for their recollections and occasional photo prompts. Likewise my sisters Lal and Fleur for theirs.

Simon Green of Blaqua has supplied me with glorious colored and patterned shirts for some years; it was he who first suggested I write a memoir—thank you, Simon. Subsequently, I must thank Kevin Pocklington who became my agent, Andreas Campomar who then became my editor, and the powers that be at Little, Brown for having the faith to become my UK publisher. Thanks also to my old friend and manager Richard Bishop for his help in the proceedings, and a heartfelt thank you

1967

to Gina Frary Bacon at Tiny Ghost in Nashville for her assistance in so many ways over the period I've been putting this story together.

I am also very grateful to my niece and nephew, Ruby and Ed Wright; and also to my dear friend Jan Clements for London Bridge accommodation while I was finishing this book.

Finally, my undying love and gratitude go to my amazing wife Emma Swift for her strength, support, and inspiration over the last ten years.